A Carpet of Blue

An Ex-Cop Takes a Tough Look
at America's Drug Problem

Tony Bouza

Deaconess Press
Minneapolis, Minnesota

To the kids, whose vulnerable honesty and heroic struggles moved me to write this book.

First Published March 1992

ISBN 0-925190-21-7
Library of Congress Catalog Card Number 91-077591

Printed in the United States of America
96 95 94 93 92   8 7 6 5 4 3 2 1

Cover design by Ned Skubic
Photography by Jerry Taube

Editor's Note: Deaconess Press publishes books and pamphlets related to the subjects of physical health, mental health, and chemical dependency. A CARPET OF BLUE and other publications do not necessarily reflect the philosophy of Fairview or Fairview Deaconess, or their treatment programs.

Acknowledgments

There is a bit of hubris about thanking others for their help. It implies that something wonderful has been produced but the author is too modest to lay claim to it. That's not how I feel. I can see the flaws of my style and the limits of my wit too clearly to claim any credit. I can also see that others really did try to help and that much of whatever merit the work has really belongs to them.

First, Tom Collins—for believing in my message, for doing something about the problems and for giving me the vehicle for the expression of some thoughts. Ed Wedman worked hard and effectively behind the scenes and took risks and even endured expenses to make this a better book. Bob Italia was generous, devoted and hardworking in capturing my voice and producing a first draft.

A Carpet of Blue

Jan Arellano was the amanuensis, critic, goad and seeker of errors that every flawed writer needs. Lane Stiles was simply the best and hardest working editor I've ever met—a statement sure to get me into a lot of trouble with others, but there it is.

That the ultimate responsibility, and blame, are mine will be only too clear from the contents. I did my best only because the folks above wouldn't let me get away with less.

Contents

Introduction

The war on drugs will decide the fate of the nation.

Right now we are losing that war.

Like most wars, this one involves many battlefields. The more obvious and frightening aspects of the war are captured in the words "crime," "guns," and "violence." But just as important are the quieter struggles being waged within families, at schools, between friends and in front of the television.

At the local level, confused and frightened communities desperately grasp for palliatives.

At the national level, an indifferent administration focuses its energies on international politics, ignoring the domestic scene.

This book looks at the drug problem from the perspective of what we are doing—mostly wrong—and what we might do to win this much-heralded but feebly prosecuted war.

Rather than seeing the drug war as a challenge that, if met, might well lead to a moral regeneration, we have mainly opted for a repressive model and hoped for the best. The result has been a continuing slide into urban chaos and social disintegration.

The war on drugs is poorly understood and ineffectively waged because of our inability to grasp its complexities and our reluctance to adopt the measures needed to succeed. The goal of this book is to try to illuminate the issues and to suggest strategies that might prove more effective.

It will not be an easy war to win. We are up against a formidable enemy. The comic strip character Pogo said it best: "We have met the enemy, and they are us." We have mainly ourselves to blame for the conditions that have spawned so much addiction, violence and crime.

A major focus of this book will be on the home. That's where we will win—or lose—the drug war. America is a collection of families. What happens to those families is what will happen to the nation.

The American family is becoming the victim of the sort of hedonism and self-absorption that overtook so many other powerful civilizations in the past. Americans seem to have lost their way. The American family has to get itself back together. It must overcome abuse, alcoholism and divorce, and return stability, structure and love into the home. These latter ingredients are in short supply today. Yes, we can send Americans to the moon and win a major war in days, but our inability to cure internal ills is mostly due to our reluctance to give up our pleasures.

Indeed, parents need to examine their nests very carefully. And they must examine their own behaviors. They must learn the difference between saying and doing. You can tell your kids all the things you want, but they will pick up on your actions. Are you telling your kids not to drink and then sitting back, watching television and downing a few beers? If you are, you're giving your kids a very clear message. The message is not "Don't drink," but "Drink."

In the early 1960s, there were about 400,000 divorces a year. Now there are 1.2 million divorces a year. (The murder and violence rates have almost exactly followed this trend.) Half of the marriages undertaken today will wind up in divorce. Why? Are there that many legitimate reasons for these staggering numbers? Or does the divorce rate have more to do with changing values and an infatuation with life's not-so-simple pleasures—a reflection of a tilt toward hedonism and away from fealty to solemn oaths?

The true victims of societal dissolution, and of the drug war, are our children. They are victims twice over—of a bleak present and an even bleaker future.

A lot of kids were interviewed for this book—kids in treatment, struggling to reclaim their lives. Some of them will make it. Some won't. Listening to their stories, I found it amazing that they refused to blame anyone but themselves for their troubles. A quick look into their lives reveals the pervasive confusion in their homes— mothers desperate to keep families together, for example, enabling their alcoholic husbands to abuse their children and themselves. The influences of peers, school and television are also apparent.

Most of these kids started abusing drugs at a very young age. One got drunk on beer and wine when only ten years old. Alcohol was freely available in the home, and everyone in the family drank. The kids' stories, while varying, assume a sameness in the repetition of patterns that attest to the moral bankruptcy of their environment and suggest a bleak landscape for their younger brothers and sisters.

We need to reexamine our values, which have shifted away from "us" towards "me." Prosperity has enabled some of us to indulge in orgies of consumerism, materialism and narcissism. Think of these "silly" old words: duty, honor, country, sacrifice, discipline. We don't use these words anymore. The ancient Egyptians, Greeks, Romans and Spaniards lost their way in a world of self-indulgence, pleasure, pomposity and decadence. To suggest that our civilization might suffer a similar decline may seem outrageous, but the idea must have seemed equally outrageous to the Egyptians, Greeks, Romans and Spaniards.

Ironies abound in history. The preeminent irony for America is that at this moment of ascendancy, when capitalism is triumphing over communism as both a political and economic idea, when the Russians have abandoned communism, when Eastern Europe has abandoned totalitarianism, when the threat that has obsessed us for half a century is suddenly dispelled, the seeds of our destruction are being sowed within.

We can see where our values have taken us by looking at those we consider heroes. Who are the best paid professionals in our society? Those who give us pleasure, who entertain us—athletes and movie stars. Who are the least paid professionals in our society?

Teachers, counselors, ministers—those who transmit worthy values. Society sets its priorities. We're willing to pay huge salaries to athletes and movie stars because entertainment is our principal value.

The drug problem correlates to this pleasure principle because drug use also represents a search for pleasure. If you listen to kids with drug problems, they'll all tell you the same thing: "Hey, I love drugs. I don't want to get off drugs. They make me feel good—and it's fun." What's most frightening about this search for pleasure through drugs is that it is resulting in increasing rates of addiction, violence and crime, especially among the underclass, posing a serious threat to the internal peace of the nation.

The national drug policy we have right now (what there is of one) isn't working. Its fundamental flaw is that it panders to our worst instincts. "You want action, we'll give you action" is what the politicians and drug law enforcers say. "We'll arrest everybody, conduct sweeps and roundups, fill the jails." More cops, more money for drug enforcement, more prisons, tougher judges, longer sentences, bigger jails. Powerful stuff. The nightly news abounds with sensational raids and drug busts. We watch in fascination. But there's a problem: such mindless "action" isn't working. The drug crisis doesn't improve, it gets worse.

The national drug policy needs to be more focused. Los Angeles does roundups and sweeps. New York freezes an area and carpets it with blue. The Midwest does partnerships with the feds and goes after higher-ups. Nothing works because there is no overriding plan or philosophy. We have no coherent policy about growers, importers or wholesalers. Instead, we do roundups and jump street collars (i.e., do small-scale buys on the street and arrest the sellers, also known as "buy-and-bust" operations) and fill our prisons with blacks and Hispanics and the poor—the users and the victims.

I draw upon my thirty-six years of police service to show how local drug enforcement policies are made, the problems with local policies, and how cops go about enforcing them. The issues of crime and violence will be examined to show from firsthand experience why a Miami Vice approach to drug control doesn't work.

In addition to analyzing these problems, I will offer suggestions to parents, local community members, educators and the members of the media on how to reverse the trends toward increasing levels of drug use and drug-related crime and violence.

The main mistake Americans have made—in the home and nationally—is to adopt the simple solutions of the demagogues who urge mindless action while ignoring the enormous complexities of human behavior. Parents are exhorted to "just say no" and to mouth platitudes. The government builds prisons and hires cops. And everyone is encouraged to ignore the social, racial, cultural, moral and economic forces that are actually driving drug use among our youth—especially in the ghetto.

The drug problem extends not only beyond the home to the national level, but internationally as well, so in this book I'll examine what we must do to stop the flow of drugs into our country. For example, how do we combat the source of the cocaine supply: the farmers growing coca? If you listen to the present administration, you burn their fields. But then what? What are you going to replace the coca with? The farmers in Colombia and Peru have families to feed. And they've been growing coca for centuries.

I watched with great anticipation as a new President was inaugurated in 1989. I was hopeful that this time we would be given a coherent, thoughtful and wide-ranging drug program, a program that recognized the scope and complexity of the drug problem, a program that began with a clear plan and followed with decisive execution. But what has President Bush offered us instead? A national drug policy that is all smoke and mirrors, gongs and cymbals. More money for overtime so that cops can get time-and-a-half to play Rambo. Round up the usual suspects, throw them into the system, say the job is done and get the folks off your back. If this policy remains in place, we will continue to lose the war—and, with it, the nation.

I would like to see the President's attention focused on the interconnections between race and poverty and drugs and crime. I would like to hear him say, "Okay, I have been spending a lot of energy looking at the big bear over the water, but now it seems to be tame. So now what? What's happening in my house? And how do I go about making effective changes here?" These are the questions we all need to ask ourselves. That's what this book is all about.

Our streets are littered with blood and violence. Guns, drugs and crime are the bywords of our age. We see the carnage downstream and demand action, but we rarely recognize that the causes of the carnage may lie upstream—in racism and poverty—and that we must either resolve these problems or resign ourselves to the continuing disintegration of our cities and our nation.

1

Losing the War

It is tempting to say we lack a national strategy to control drugs, but that's not true. We do have a national strategy. It only seems we don't because the strategy isn't working.

Devised by President George Bush and his former "drug czar," William Bennett, and released by the White House in January, 1990, the National Drug Control Strategy is based on the cynical assumption that Americans want mindless action in the war against drugs and are eager for simplistic—even draconian—solutions. The President's strategy favors telegenic enforcement procedures like police sweeps, roundups and buy-and-bust street operations over less "popular" but more promising and substantial approaches like research, education, prevention and treatment. Typical of President Bush's cynical soundbyte approach to the drug problem was his televised speech to the nation on September 5, 1989. During the speech, President Bush held up a glassene envelope containing white powder and solemnly announced that it had been purchased under the shadow of the White House in Lafayette Park. Later we learned that the seller didn't even know where Lafayette Park was and that the federal agents who arrested him had had the devil's own time guiding him to the desired location. Bush's speech was just another public relations ploy to hawk the snake oil of a seductive but ultimately ineffectual drug policy.

Conservatives like Bush and Bennett favor tough enforcement measures that are the domestic equivalents of their tough international policies of a strong and aggressive military. When liberals advocate social welfare and reform programs, they are accused of being touchy-feely, of throwing green at the drug problem. Conservatives, on the other hand, are rarely criticized when they throw blue (i.e., cops) at the drug problem. Today's political climate clearly favors the more conservative "lock 'em up" approach.

The focus on enforcement has resulted in the channeling of enormous amounts of federal monies into paid time-and-a-half for overtime police programs that produce constitutionally and strategically suspect round-ups, sweeps, saturation zones and other low-level—but telegenic—street operations. New York lays down a carpet of blue to displace crime; Los Angeles sweeps up street gangs; Minneapolis joins the feds in an effort to strike at higher level dealers. The different approaches intersect in a confusing and uncertain maze in which the only constant is an undiminished supply of drugs at low cost.

The National Drug Control Strategy distills the views of many experts from many levels of society. But as the introduction by William Bennett makes clear, the experts speak with one voice. The key word is enforcement. Those with alternative points of view are labeled "cynics and defeatists." Anecdotes describing the heroic efforts of a few community activists are offered as proof that progress is being made in the war against drugs, when clearly that is not the case. Considerable energy is spent on demolishing the straw man of decriminalization, when only a benighted few have embraced the notion of legalizing hard drugs.

The President calls drugs "the gravest domestic threat facing our nation today." But enforcement is the only word in the strategy document not followed by a but. And although former drug czar Bennett once served as Secretary of Education under Ronald Reagan, education forms an insignificant part of the overall drug control plan.

The National Drug Control Strategy funnels about ten billion dollars a year into what amounts to little more than building new jails, hiring more judges and prosecutors, and paying overtime for cops. Specifically, in the area of criminal justice, the plan advocates more and better prepared and supported federal enforcement agents, more help for local federal task forces, funding to increase investigations into money laundering, more judges and other court personnel, more investigators for organized crime/drug trafficking operations, more funds for local cops, improved drug testing capability and more investigations of local marijuana growing. The plan cites street-level enforcement as the most effective tactic against drug abuse.

11

A potpourri of federal agencies is charged with fanning out across the drug spectrum to bring their particular expertise to bear on a given aspect of the drug problem. The Drug Enforcement Agency (DEA), for example, targets the high-level drug operators, nation-

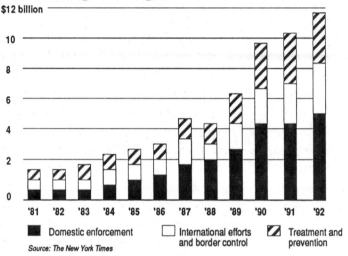

The Drug War's Growing Budget

Obligated budget allocations for fiscal years through 1990, Congressionally enacted spending for 1991, and the Administration's budget request for 1992.

Domestic enforcement

International efforts and border control

Treatment and prevention

Source: The New York Times

ally and internationally. The Federal Bureau of Investigation (FBI) tackles drug dealing connected with organized crime. The Bureau of Alchohol, Tobacco and Firearms focuses on gun-related drug crimes. And the Department of the Treasury concentrates on money laundering and transfers of large sums of money. All of these agencies receive additional funds under the National Drug Control Strategy.

A total of 9.5 billion dollars was requested for national drug control for the fiscal year 1990. Of that total, 3.8 billion was for the Department of Justice, 800 million for the Treasury Department, 700 million for the Coast Guard, 300 million for the State Department, 877 million for the Defense Department, 271 million for the Department of Veteran's Affairs and 324 million to the courts. Over seven billion dollars was requested for enforcement, with just one dollar in four left over for prevention, education, research and treatment.

It is clear that these vital areas are being short-changed for the sort of sexy enforcement techniques that look good on the nightly news. While the President's approach includes the usual pieties about prevention, education, research and treatment, it allocates the lion's share of actual resources to law enforcement—an approach that produces a deluge of arrests and jailings in an already flooded judicial system. The few funds dedicated to prevention, education, research and treatment are aimed primarily at the middle class rather than the harder to reach urban underclass, where the need is much greater. One of the results is a judicial system with growing waiting lists of applicants for treatment programs. Judges throw up their hands in despair at their inability to order offenders into treatment, and this at a time when the connection between drugs and criminality is recognized to be so profound and extensive that even sex offenders are given a chemical dependency evaluation as the first step in their treatment.

It is not until deep into the report that the dread subject of education is taken up in any substance, in a section entitled "Community Action and the Workplace." This section deals with school and community-based prevention programs, programs targeted at high-risk children, drugs in public housing, cooperative programs between feds and the corporate sector, drug-free workplaces, federal employee assistance programs, and steroid and licit drug abuse.

(This last area—steroid and licit drug abuse—reminds us how transient, shifting and faddish the specific drugs of choice can be. Today's hot drug quickly becomes passe as another more alluring drug takes its place.)

The impression left by this slighting of education is of an administration that doesn't put a lot of faith in "soft," amorphous, long-term anti-drug efforts. The preference is clearly for "hard" street action, rather than a carefully wrought national program that flows from a reasoned analysis of the problem.

Still, with many Americans in a near state of panic over the prevalance of drugs and crime in their neighborhoods, the President, in spite of a decided predilection for the quick fix, is obligated to produce a program that at least appears to touch all the bases. Therefore his plan also pays lip service to a number of international initiatives, including economic, military and law enforcement assistance to Columbia, Bolivia and Peru; cooperation with Mexico in various money/drug operations; law enforcement assistance for those South American countries involved in the growing and transporting of drugs; cooperative law enforcement and intelligence operations with Central American and Caribbean nations; international strategies for controlling opium and heroin, money laundering, and the production of the chemicals used to manufacture illegal drugs; and other international agreements for the control of drugs.

The call for the development of a strategy for opium and heroin is surprising in the sense that it implies that a similar strategy for, say, cocaine already exists, or that one for, say, marijuana isn't needed. It is also surprising, coming as it does from an administration that prefers to act on its impulses, that it does acknowledge, however obliquely, that long-term strategies are needed.

This administration is most comfortable when talking about enforcement and the hardware that enforcement entails. The administration's report posits the potentially dangerous idea of increased military involvement in the control of drugs. Certainly there is a need for a sensible program of interdiction, but for a hundred years Americans have been very hesitant to use the military in domestic law enforcement actions. Yet the President's plan expresses no equivocations or doubts about this issue. The message is clear: involve the military and make its operations more efficient. That we have never assigned domestic law enforcement activities to our armed forces doesn't trouble these planners in the least. Any solution that promises quick, dramatic action is embraced. Political expediency sets the agenda.

The war on drugs has been fought as a series of skirmishes uninformed by any grand vision or unified tactics. What the anti-drug campaign has lacked is a coherent plan around which the disparate groups of combatants might coalesce. The development of such a plan would require many months of concentrated study by a task force that would survey what was known, analyze what was needed and develop a single coherent long-range plan. What the President has offered instead is a laundry list of approaches that attempts to cover too much with too little discrimination and that places too much emphasis on enforcement over prevention, education, research and treatment.

The President's plan does call for some research, but there is a notable absence of the sort of bold proposals needed to develop a body of knowledge on which to found a comprehensive national plan that the American community might rally around. Bush's research agenda would address only a few of the multitudinous pieces of the vast and complex drug mosaic.

Intelligence—the gathering and compilation of information—is another area that gets short shrift in the National Drug Control Strategy. The report does call for the creation of a national data center to serve as a repository for information on drug trafficking, but overall this critically important area gets just two pages of consideration in an 85-page report, another example of the way the administration tiptoes around touchy questions. Intelligence gathering has fallen out of favor because of numerous recent abuses. Watergate, Iran-Contra, various activities of the CIA and the FBI, and periodic police scandals around the country have spooked bureaucrats away from intelligence gathering, even by legitimate and legal means. The baby of intelligence is being thrown out with the bathwater of potential abuse. It is absolutely necessary that police agencies continue to gather data aggressively—through legal means and subject to the oversight of elected officials. (Sadly, many people no longer trust our elected officials to oversee the gathering of intelligence responsibly.)

Overall, the National Drug Control Strategy reflects a studied contempt for long-term upstream approaches (i.e., approaches that take into account the root causes of drug abuse, such as poverty and racism) and an over-reliance on more punitive, short-term downstream approaches. But why not? This is the same administration that pandered to white American racism by demonizing a black criminal, Willie Horton, in the 1988 presidential election.

So how does this report translate into action on the streets? In different ways, but with the same result. Some police agencies do one thing, others do other things, but all fall short of solving the problem. In every case, the emphasis is on attacking the sort of street-level crime that is so visible and upsetting to the average citizen but which represents the lowest and least important rung of the drug trafficking ladder. Rather than solving the problem, the arrests merely exacerbate it by flooding the criminal justice system with impoverished addicts and low-level dealers. Frequently, since operations tend to center in the poorest sections of our cities, those arrested are people of color, especially blacks. The war on drugs becomes by default a racist war on people of color, filling our jails with the minnows of the drug trade while the sharks swim freely away.

The public panic induced by drugs and crime has brought enormous pressure on the criminal justice system to attack the more visible manifestations of the problem. It would seem that the public just wants to see the corner dealer led off in chains to jail and is unconcerned about the importer or wholesaler it cannot see. Worse, the dominant society seems to feel little compunction about the constitutional niceties of search and seizure or the legality of arrests when it comes to drug dealers, particularly when those drug dealers are ghetto dwellers, people of color or members of the underclass. Even the liberal columnist Sydney Schanberg has called for the imposition of a state of emergency and the suspension of certain constitutional rights as frills we can no longer afford in the war on drugs.

American racial and economic injustices create an underclass that seeks to escape its miseries through any means available—often drugs. The use of and trafficking in such substances as alcohol, cocaine, heroin, crack, marijuana, and PCP is inextricably bound up with criminality. The tragic result is that a higher percentage of black men are incarcerated in the United States today than in South Africa. A study undertaken by the Sentencing Project in Washington, D.C. revealed that one in four black men in their twenties was either in jail or prison, on parole or on probation. Only one in every seventeen white males in their twenties was under the same sort of control.

Increasing penalties and imposing mandatory sentences for drug dealing has made plea bargaining—an essential and misunderstood feature of the system—less common, thereby burdening the courts with trials they cannot and should not be conducting. This is another example of how simple-minded, "get tough" tactics can backfire. The criminal justice system has the resources to try only a small percentage of the criminal cases it must process—perhaps no more than five percent. Plea bargaining keeps the cases flowing. (Problems can arise, however, when politically ambitious or insecure prosecutors bargain hastily, accepting light sentences for drug dealers in order to fatten their conviction rate "batting averages." The entire system then becomes vulnerable to criticism, especially in an election year.)

As a consequence of public pressures for visible action, arrests for the sale and manufacture of illegal drugs rose from 100,000 in 1980 to 400,000 in 1989 and arrests for simple possession jumped from 368,000 in 1980 to 843,000 in 1989. The increasing volume of arrests burdens a system that has limited most of its expansion to hiring more cops. Parenthetically, it is interesting to note that this increase occurred during a period in which conservatives were complaining that decisions by the Supreme Court were "handcuffing" the police.

The police, perhaps sensing the ineffectiveness of a one-dimensional enforcement approach, have initiated educational programs like DARE (Drug Awareness Resistance Education). DARE puts cops into classrooms to talk to kids about the dangers of drug use and how to avoid them. But what police really need is a national strategy on drugs as comprehensive and forward-thinking as was President Lyndon Johnson's Report on Crime in 1967. The current strategy contains nothing new. It doesn't even build on what we already know. We need to do more.

What's the easiest thing to do when you want to go after drug dealers? Go out into the street and do buy-and-bust operations. What's the hardest thing to do? Catch the really sophisticated dealers—the importers and wholesalers. To do that, you must wind your way through an elaborate labyrinth of interlocking organizations and individuals. The drug kingpins have tremendous resources. They can hire expensive lawyers. They can afford to insulate themselves from direct involvement with drugs. It takes a lot of time and energy to get at them, so to get quick results police chiefs tend to concentrate on highly visible street sweeps and to neglect the more expensive and time consuming investigations of higher-ups. That's a big mistake. You're much better off making a seizure of 200 pounds of cocaine and arresting the person who is importing the drug than you are arresting 200 dealers who are selling one pound each. The simple math of the equation seems to have eluded many law enforcers.

Members of the underclass are the ones who are most often swept up by law enforcement because they are the ones who are most likely to be operating publicly on the streets (rather than privately in suburban homes). What does the police chief hear? "They're selling drugs in the street!" "They're selling drugs in my neighborhood!" "They're selling drugs openly by the school! What are you going to do about it?"

When I was police chief in Minneapolis from 1980 through 1988, my answer was: "I'm going to concentrate on the higher-ups." I got into a lot of difficulty over it. I did indeed go after the higher-ups, which meant I could not devote as much energy to street operations as some people wanted. Instead, I worked with the feds and focused on the bigger dealers—like Casey Ramirez.

People imagine drug dealers as monsters—specifically, as dehumanized representatives of the underclass, a la Willie Horton. They tend to accept uncritically the Hollywood stereotype of the villain. In truth, drug dealers can be as charming, attractive, and affable as anyone else, and they aren't, of course, necessarily members of the underclass.

Casey Ramirez was a respected benefactor of the small Minnesota town of Princeton. He called himself a philanthropist and gave money to the city to refurbish its city hall and to buy new police cars. There was even talk about planting palm trees in a hot house.

The people of Princeton never questioned their good luck. Ramirez said that he had come to Princeton because it was a nice town in which to raise a family. He was young, charming, delightful—a civic-minded, community-oriented individual and an apparent model citizen. Nobody asked about the sources of his income. In America, all that matters is how much money you have, not where you got it.

What the people of Princeton didn't know was that by the time that Ramirez arrived in their city he was already a big-time drug dealer. He did not simply come to Minnesota and start up a drug operation. The drug operation was already in existence, and Ramirez brought it with him.

I knew nothing of Casey Ramirez when we first tapped into his drug network. Minneapolis had its own drug problem, and the Minneapolis police were working with the feds to tackle it. Minneapolis undercover cops, like cops across the United States, were performing buy-and-bust operations in the streets—but with a difference. Minneapolis police would catch one street dealer and threaten to put him in jail unless he revealed the name of his supplier. The dealer would then introduce the undercover cop to the supplier, and then the supplier would be arrested.

Up this ladder of arrests and informants, we slowly climbed the drug pyramid. As we got higher up, we began to narrow our focus. "Well, there's a dealer in Princeton." "I think my supplier may get it from a guy in Princeton." "The rumor is that a guy in Princeton is running the whole show." As you get higher up, rumors begin to get more solid.

We continued our street operations and undercover work with the feds. Sometimes the investigation would lead us out of the state. For example, we had to fly Minneapolis cops to Florida to make a buy. We also did wiretaps. The same name kept coming up: Ramirez.

Sooner or later we were going to catch him. Sooner or later he would have to touch either the cash or the drugs or both. Some of the transactions involved millions of dollars. Whom could Ramirez trust with that kind of money? Any narcotics deal involving large amounts of cash requires some hands-on management. Finally, the cash and the drug trail led to Ramirez, and he was arrested quietly at home without a struggle.

I never met Casey Ramirez—never saw his face. My style as a police executive was to visualize what was going on and make plans. I operated well at the abstract level. I would call in detectives and ask about the case: "What's going on? What have you done so far?" I visualized the entire case from beginning to end. I had a feeling for what needed to be done. The clutter and distractions of actual crime scenes could obscure the truth. Functioning as a spider at the center of a web— that was my style.

Casey Ramirez was eventually brought to trial. He retained a very sharp and expensive attorney. It was a full-scale trial—no guilty plea, no negotiated arrangements. After a long and difficult proceeding, Casey Ramirez was found guilty. He and his lawyer could not overcome the mountains of physical evidence stacked up against him.

The lawyer ended up with half of Ramirez's wealth. The Minneapolis Police Department confiscated the other half. Ramirez ended up in prison with a long sentence.

But Ramirez didn't end up in prison alone. Some of the "upstanding" neighbors that he had befriended—and used—ended up in prison with him—or else became witnesses for the government against him. Many others resisted the accusations against Ramirez to the very end. The case was not unlike that of another drug kingpin, named William F. LaMorte, who similarly bamboozled local communities in Connecticut and New York with such acts of civic generosity as throwing parties for law enforcement officials and sponsoring public fireworks displays. In both cases, local citizens not only accepted the benevolence of these men without question but were even angered when the government brought charges of drug dealing against them. The double standard here is obvious. By aping the values of the overclass and pandering to the greed of the dominant community, drug kingpins like Ramirez and LaMorte can operate without suspicion—can even be admired and defended, while small-time street dealers, particularly blacks and other minorities, are excoriated and condemned without a second thought.

I knew that my approach to drug control made me vulnerable to political attack. My priorities were to go after the higher-ups—wherever that led. An aggressive, wide-ranging inquiry could take us anywhere, including South America and Europe. I had made up my mind how I was going to conduct drug investigations because I could justify the operations on a logical basis.

There was only one problem: the Minneapolis City Council.

The highly publicized Ramirez case brought to the Council's attention my aggressive style of pursuing the higher-ups anywhere and everywhere.

The Council President in particular criticized me severely, knowing that she was playing on the parochialism of her colleagues and constituents.

"What are Minneapolis cops doing in Princeton arresting Casey Ramirez when they should be policing the streets of our city?" she asked. "Do you know what it says on their badges? It says "Minneapolis Police Department." The taxpayers of this city are paying for them!"

"Do you think that Casey Ramirez's only market was Princeton, Minnesota?" I replied. "If he is importing drugs into the state, don't you think he might be selling them in Minneapolis? If you want to stop cocaine trafficking in the city, you've got to go to places like Miami and Princeton."

That was a very difficult connection for her to make. She wanted Minneapolis cops kept in Minneapolis. Local politicians tend to be very parochial and xenophobic. They're paying the bills and they want everything centered in the city. But the police, already scattered and fragmented among literally thousands of cities and towns, are further hamstrung when they are not allowed to pursue leads beyond the borders of their jurisdictions.

Local politicians tend to believe that they're police experts, that they know best about police procedures and policies. To them, a police chief is merely a member of the staff. But that doesn't make any sense whatsoever. I was the professional they had hired to run the police department. Yet they could hardly resist the temptation to tell me exactly how to do my job. They recognized neither the depth of my task nor the shallowness of their opinions.

The Council President saw the Ramirez case as a perfect opportunity to attack my policies. She picked the issue carefully. She felt that her criticisms would be supported by the other members of the Council. But her assumption proved to be wrong. The rest of the Council reluctantly approved my decisions.

The Mayor was more than satisfied with my aggressive tactics, and was very supportive. He knew that I had been running a very aggressive operation against Ramirez because I had briefed him throughout the investigation.

The opposition of the Council President to my

policies was—and continues to be—indicative of a widespread preference among shortsighted politicians for small-scale, highly visible, local street arrests. Ignored, at great risk, is the hidden menace lurking behind these corner dealers. We must treat the causes as well as the symptoms, or the disease will never be cured.

The trail of drugs does not begin and end on the streets of America. Its source may be thousands of miles away in an impoverished third world country like Afghanistan. It may begin with a poor Afghan farmer who owns little land and has few crops that he can raise on that land. What the farmer does have is a large family to feed. Growing poppies is a logical choice for him. Poppies are a hardy plant, and the farmer can make a lot of cash selling them.

So the Afghan farmer plants the poppies and tends to them. When the plants mature, he makes a small incision in them and the plants bleed sap—like tapping a maple tree, except that this sap produces opium, morphine and heroin instead of syrup.

The poor farmer then sells the sap to a local businessman who refines it chemically into pure heroin. The local businessman now must get the heroin to the lucrative illicit drug markets outside his country. Enter the importer. Frequently, the importer will be a European whose familiarity with European custom practices and contacts in European seaports allow him to straddle the borders of international trade.

In order to transport the heroin to overseas markets, smugglers (also called mules) are needed. Smuggling techniques can be ingenious, but they are often very risky too. Swallowers, for example, are smugglers who conceal heroin by stuffing it inside a condom and swallowing it. Sometimes the condom breaks and the heroin leaks out, killing the swallower.

Once the drug gets past customs or gets flown to a remote airport or beached on a lonely shore, the importer sells it to a distributor. The distributor then "cuts" the raw drug, i.e., dilutes it by mixing it with some cheap neutral chemical, and sells it on the streets to a user who often is a street dealer himself. The person who finally consumes the drug may end up getting 99% sugar and only 1% heroin, but the kick is still there.

The cocaine chain works similarly. Both powdered cocaine and rock cocaine, or crack, come from the coca plant that grows naturally in the Andes Mountains of Peru, Colombia and Bolivia. The natives of these countries have been chewing coca leaf for centuries. Chewing the leaves produces a calming euphoric effect, much milder than the effect produced by sniffing, injecting or smoking the pure extracted drug.

The coca leaves are sold by South American farmers to local businessmen who convert the crop into a cocaine base that is exported mostly to the United States. In 1990, Peruvian farmers were typically receiving about $350 for the 500 pounds of coca leaves that would be processed into a single pound of pure cocaine worth $45,000 on American streets. The enormous markup in price is related to the risks of drug trafficking rather than the cost of production. Drug entrepeneurs willing to take on the risks stand to make enormous profits. This is how the powerful drug cartels were born.

Where in this long drug chain should police focus their enforcement efforts? As I noted earlier, police are under pressure to attack the drug problem where the public sees it most plainly—on the city streets, around the schools, in the neighborhoods. That's the easiest place to attack the problem. You get a sallow-complexioned cop to dress like a strung-out junkie. He hangs out on the street and buys drugs from dealers. Then he alerts a detective, points out the dealer and says: "I just bought $3.00 worth of crack from that jerk over there." And the detective walks over to the dealer and arrests him. The cop keeps on making buys until his identity is revealed. After he is "burned," the cop comes into the courts to testify against all the dealers he has fingered.

Testifying in open court forces an undercover cop to burn his cover. Once a cop's identity is blown, so is his usefulness as an undercover buyer of illicit drugs. Naturally, the police prefer to burn as few undercover cops as possible. Therefore, if a dealer pleads not guilty and is subsequently convicted in court, he can expect a lot stiffer sentence than he would have gotten had he accepted a plea bargain from the District Attorney. Under this system of retribution against those who insist upon a trial, very few undercover cops have to be burned. They can stay on the street and continue to make "jump collar" after "jump collar."

The trouble with this system is that we always wind up striking at the low-level user and buyer, and we flood the system with arrests while the major players—the processor, the importer, the distributor—go untouched. This policy does not serve the public well. It panders to people's fears without providing them any real relief or safety.

In 1989, the Police Chief of Washington, D.C. announced that his police force had made 43,000 narcotics-related arrests in two years because of a special program that focused on street conditions related to drugs. He was very proud of his accomplishments. But soon after the announcement, the system began to crack under the strain of so many arrests and quickly collapsed. Despite the Chief's boasting, what he had really done was to cripple Washington's criminal justice system by overloading it with low-level buy-and-bust arrests. He tried to use the statistics to claim that he was doing something substantial about the drug problem. (In 1990, he ran for mayor and lost.) But in 1989 and 1990, Washington, D.C., America's most policed city, had the highest murder rate in the nation—and many of those murders were drug-related. When the city tested the urine of suspects arrested on the streets, it found that fully three fourths of the suspects showed traces of felony drugs.

Drug enforcement strategies are too fragmented to be effective on a national level. Each major city in America seems to have its own way of attacking drugs. Los Angeles takes a very militaristic approach. Los Angeles has a serious street gang problem, and the LAPD has responded with tough, aggressive street tactics that include sweeps, roundups and vigorous patrols.

Chicago also experiences serious gang violence and turf battles for the control of the drug trade, to which it responds on several levels. Basically, the Chicago Police fight a two-front war—against drug traffic and against gangs involved in drugs and violence. Chicago engages both local uniformed and plainclothes forces, as well as higher level headquarters units, some of which work closely with the feds, in its war against drugs.

Put simply, Los Angeles's is a militaristic, impersonal, gung ho tradition of aggressive patrolling, while Chicago's approach is more sociologically and community oriented.

New York City has attempted to address the drug problem through programs like "Operation Pressure Point," which covered the lower east side with cops in order to inhibit drug dealing and other crimes in the streets. The NYPD carpeted an entire community with blue and shut down illicit street activities. But what they really did was make a wilderness and call it peace. Even though this one particular area was pacified, in the end the hundreds of cops only managed to displace the drug activity to other parts of the city. The gentrifiers who owned property in the area loved Operation Pressure Point, but the problem wasn't fixed—it just moved down the street. Crime displacement is not crime prevention.

A critical link in the drug chain for law enforcement is the importer. That's where you can intercept the largest quantities of drugs. But in order to get to the importer, you've got to climb the drug ladder. You've got to infiltrate, do wiretaps. You have to conduct a very sophisticated, very costly, very lengthy investigation. When you arrest a user, you've got to say, "Okay, I want your seller. Take me with you the next time you make a buy and introduce me as your buddy. Then I'll buy some stuff from him." The user has to go along with you or else go to prison. That's an easy choice to make. So the user takes you with him, and you buy from his seller, and you arrest the seller. Then you say, "Okay, who are you getting your stuff from? If you cooperate with me, we'll go easier on you—maybe even make a deal." So now you get the name of the dealer's seller, and you're getting closer to the importer.

To climb the ladder all the way to the top, local law enforcement agencies must develop partnerships with the feds. Task forces can be formed in cooperation with the Drug Enforcement Administration, for example. The DEA essentially runs the investigation. They have the supervisors, the money, the personnel and the equipment. Local law enforcement agencies contribute anywhere from three to twenty cops who work with the feds with the understanding that the focus will be on local drug dealing, although the investigation may take them anywhere in the country—or beyond.

It isn't easy. America has 15,000 police departments. As soon as you leave your city, you're dealing with another police department, and police departments don't always communicate with each other like they should. One way to overcome this problem is to join in partnerships with police agencies that have national jurisdiction, such as the FBI, the DEA, and the Treasury Department.

What we need to do is to develop a truly strategic plan on the national level. We need to appoint a presidential commission on drug abuse and give them at least eighteen months to study the problem. Should we give the Afghan farmer aid to plant alternative crops? Should we assist foreign governments who are battling large drug cartels? Is Columbia's experiment with a partial amnesty for drug barons a daring, imaginative innovation or a cowardly, self-serving surrender? Should we establish trade bans against those countries that refuse to enforce drug restrictions or prosecute drug traffickers? What about extradition treaties with those countries that are sensitive to issues of political sovereignty? Should we, as some have suggested, unilaterally intervene by sending special weapons assault teams into the growing areas of foreign countries? Should we alter our currency, calling in all $100 bills and creating a second system of exchange? How do we prevent the importation of drugs? And once the drugs are in the country, how do we disrupt the distribution system? If we do jump collars, what do we do with the offenders once they're in the system? What do we do with the users who get busted? What do we do about the seemingly limitless demand for drugs in this nation? What about prevention, education, research and treatment?

Right now we don't have a clearly focused, coherent national policy that addresses these broad questions. Our current drug policy has more to do with the electability of public officials than it has to do with addressing the substance of the drug problem. The only thing that we have agreed on for certain is that we're losing the war on drugs.

2

On the Streets of America

The root causes of crime on the streets of America are to be found in racism and poverty. Drugs are the fuel that feeds this criminality.

Although the use of illicit drugs by white upper and middle class Americans certainly creates societal problems, of greater concern is the use of drugs by a restive underclass that is mugging, robbing, burglarizing, assaulting and killing people—often its own members—at increasing rates.

That members of the underclass are often driven to such acts by the conditions of life imposed on them by an exploitive overclass is an equation that few Americans want to complete. It is far

33

easier to deal punitively with the results of an unjust system than it is to reform that system.

Establishing the extent of the drug problem is a tricky business, made even trickier by the fact that tastes change and trends shift even as the problem is being studied. No one knows for sure how many addicts there are, or which drugs they're addicted to. Polls have been taken, employees screened, admissions to hospitals studied, overdose deaths analyzed, and prisoners' urine tested. Estimates of illicit drug users range into the millions, but any figures would have to be treated with caution.

There is one thing that police executives have long been convinced of, however, and that is the connection between drug use and street crime. Surveys show that three out of four state prisoners and jail inmates have used drugs and that more than four out of five youths in juvenile detention have used drugs. A recent National Institute of Justice study revealed that in 1984, about 35% of adult arrestees had cocaine in their systems. In mid-1988, the figure rose to 60%, and it peaked at 67% in May 1989. By September 1989, the percentage began to decline, falling to about 57% in mid-1990. In New York City, the figure was 40% in 1984, and over 80% by 1986 when the crack epidemic reached its zenith, then fell to the current 70%. These figures attest to the intimate connection between drug use and street crime.

By most measures the cocaine epidemic, which began in the early eighties, peaked in 1986. Cocaine use has been declining since. Current estimates place the number of casual users of cocaine at approximately 8 million. This number also includes 2.2 million frequent or heavy users, many of whom are addicted to crack. Rates of murder and violence related to cocaine use and trafficking continue to escalate, however. And the number of babies impaired or addicted at birth because of their mother's use of drugs continues to be very high. The reported declines in illicit drug use which our drug czar has trumpeted so confidently are more indicative of the abandonment of hard drugs by the better educated and more affluent sectors of our society. The underclass is more heavily involved in hard drugs than ever.

The cycle of drug use passes through phases of seduction (the user is attracted to the promise of pleasure without consequences), immersion (the user becomes absorbed in the drug and its culture), and disillusion (the user begins to experience more negative consequences than pleasure from the drug). Those users who are economically and socially mobile and who are well educated can more easily move through and out of this cycle, if only into another cycle, as they seek a safer route to pleasure. Members of the underclass are more likely to remain stuck in a cycle, no matter how disillusioned they become. This is what has happened with cocaine and crack use in our country.

Members of the underclass, of course, are not the only victims of the drug war. Even cops can become casualties, as was made evident in an April 8, 1990, article in *The New York Times*. Cops are constantly tempted by their proximity to drugs and drug money, and some have succumbed to the temptation. The *Times* article contained the personal account of just such a cop. His story featured the usual cast: a father who drinks and dies young, and a son who seeks refuge in alcohol and drugs. The cop's story was laced with anecdotes reflecting the double dangers of temptation and opportunity that cops are faced with. The drugs are out on the table; the urge to escape various pressures rises insistently within. Friends and fellow cops feed and reinforce his habit. Escalating addiction plunges the young cop into economic ruin as he spends all his money on drugs. In his frenetic decline, he robs crack dealers at gunpoint, sells his gun, badge and car, even pawns his sneakers to feed his habit. Finally, he is fired, and winds up in treatment.

The frightening thing about this cop's case was how bizzare his behavior had become before he was caught, which raises the question of how concerned his department was—or any other police department is—about recognizing and exposing drug use in the ranks. Are there other cops with similar problems who are going undetected?

When the Police Chief of Brockton, Massachusetts resigned in November, 1990, following the disclosure that he'd been using cocaine daily for five years and had allegedly stolen drugs from the department's evidence room, a shudder swept through the town. The Chief had spent countless hours lecturing on the evils of drugs. He seemed the least likely person in town to have a drug problem. If this paragon of virtue could succumb to drugs, who was safe from the threat?

The results of random testing suggest that the percentage of cops who use illicit drugs is small, but drug abuse does happen. It's an occupational hazard. The pressures on police officers are tremendous. Cops' experiences might be reasonably likened to those of Holocaust survivors. If you ask victims of the Holocaust about their experiences, they don't just tell you what happened, they begin to suffer all the emotions. Why? Because they have seen the human animal at its absolute worst—with no constraints and no sympathy. They know that something dark and evil lurks in the human spirit. Cops share this knowledge. Cops see the human animal at its worst—abusive, destructive, victimizing. Such knowledge is a terrible burden to carry through life. And that's why chemical abuse among cops is not uncommon. Virtually every police department has some sort of stress management and wellness program whose principal raison d'etre is to treat alcohol and drug addiction.

While I was Chief of the Minneapolis Police Department, the problem of police drug use surfaced there. I wasn't surprised. As I noted above, drug use by cops is not uncommon—though not so much narcotics and other hard drugs as alcohol.

I began to learn about the police drug problem in Minneapolis because of my open-door policy. I opened all my own mail, took my own telephone calls—my home phone was even listed in the telephone book. I was very accessible. If something happened in the department, I heard about it.

Once, one of my cops was allegedly seen smoking marijuana at a party. The word got back to me, and I called him in and had him tested for drugs. Traces of marijuana were found in his urine. I suspended him from duty. This was a very aggressive approach, but I was determined to make the police the servants of the law, not its masters.

Another time, cocaine was found in the steering wheel of a squad car. Again the offender was called in.

"Okay, buddy," I told him, "we got you. You're gonna get fired and go to jail. But maybe we can help you. Do a deal. Who else is using drugs?" He gave us names. One name led to another.

The surprising aspect of this case was the fact that other cops reported it. When it comes to internal affairs, cops usually are tightlipped. The only reason my officers reported to me in this case was because they were afraid that I had planted the drugs to test them. They knew that I had been involved in several highly publicized integrity tests of this sort while I served with the New York Police Department. So they decided to protect themselves by reporting the drugs.

Cops tend to be secretive and self-protective. A code of silence permeates police departments. It's almost like dealing with the Mafia. Cops are good liars, too. They're taught to lie. A good undercover cop has to lie. "Are you a cop?" "No." "What are you?" "I'm a junkie, just like you." The cynicism and toughness of cops have been the subjects of many studies and reports. The recent wave of police brutality incidents, from Long Beach to Los Angeles to New York, illustrates this mentality. Many police chiefs, especially those risen from the ranks they supervise, identify with the rank and file and myopically protect their officers, even to the point of covering up their wrongdoings. Prosecutors are only too familiar with the difficulty of winning a conviction against a cop even when the evidence against that cop is substantial.

Some New York State police unions have sided with the interests of their members over those of the public they are supposed to serve by supporting a bill that forbids police departments to fire officers who fail drug tests. Amazingly, the bill has passed the State Legislature-

-the same legislative body that not so long ago enthusiastically passed the nation's toughest state drug laws. Under the bill, cops would stay on the job to enforce laws they themselves had broken. So much for zero tolerance. And so much for The New York State Legislature's draconian "get tough" approach to illicit drugs.

During my nine year tenure in Minneapolis, about twenty officers were fired or disciplined for the use of hard drugs. A vastly greater number were involved in alcohol abuse, but because drinking is more socially acceptable, violations were harder to prove.

The public's reaction to the firings of cops for drug use was interesting. There was relative silence. That's the way the public reacts when they think you're taking care of business.

The cops, on the other hand, thought I was a cruel, vicious, evil monster who had absolutely no sympathy for their views. It didn't matter what it was that I caught them doing. They didn't like me to wash their dirty linen in public. They had never fully accepted the notion of a public office as a public trust. I had.

There is a lot of pressure within departments to ignore anonymous tips and letters, but they frequently point the way to a problem. Because citizens fear reprisals, they will often only report wrongdoings by police anonymously. The position of most police unions is that an anonymous charge should not be dignified with a formal inquiry, but the determined police administrator knows that he has to kick over every rock if he is going to keep his department clean. How a police administrator responds to anonymous charges against his officers often determines whether problems are uncovered and addressed or merely papered over and ignored.

It is critical that workers in safety-sensitive positions like law enforcement be drug-free. Random testing is one way of insuring this. No one wants cops, train engineers or pilots to be doing drugs, and yet our daily news accounts reveal that this is happening.

The use of illegal drugs not only produces crime on the streets of America but creates other kinds of social misery as well. One study by the Federal Center for Disease Control found an extraordinarily high incidence of AIDS among black women due to contaminated needles and unsafe sex practices like prostitution and unprotected sex with infected drug users. This is not only a tragedy for the women who acquire the disease, but also for the babies they produce. Nationally, the AIDS rate for black women is nine times that for white women, and a significant amount of this can be attributed to drug use—drug use rooted in poverty and racism.

But we have to be careful not to oversimplify the problem or to accept simplistic stereotypes. For example, a study funded by the Rockefeller Foundation and the Rand Corporation found that many street dealers held legitimate jobs and spent less than four hours a day selling cocaine. They typically made $30 an hour selling drugs—$24,000 to $43,000 annually. Since a normal sales day lasted only from 6:00 p.m. to 10:00 p.m., the "part-time" dealers were able to hold down full-time day jobs as construction workers, delivery men, office clerks and cooks. More than three fourths of the dealers studied used drugs themselves.

Poverty By Racial Group

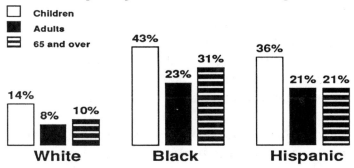

Percentage of each group living below the poverty level in 1989
Source: The New York Times

This "respectable" face of the drug problem was reinforced by another study, conducted by Smith Kline Beecham Clinical Laboratories, which found that of nearly a million workers tested for drugs in the first six months of 1990, 13.8% showed positive. The most frequently detected drugs were cocaine (21.8%) and marijuana (39%).

Every study adds another piece to the complex mosaic that makes up our national drug problem. Drug use and drug-inspired crime and violence are very complex behaviors done for a variety of motives by people in dramatically different circumstances. Unfortunately, these studies are too rare, too sporadic, too narrow and too isolated. We need more research, but we are only getting more jails, judges and cops.

On June 19, 1991, the Director of the Office of National Drug Control Policy, Bob Martinez, said in a speech that Americans spent an estimated $40 billion on cocaine, heroin, marijuana and other illegal drugs in 1990. This figure reflects a sharp decline from the $51.6

billion spent on illicit drugs in 1988 and the $49.8 billion spent in 1989. These figures are supported in recent polls of graduating high school seniors and in other statistics cited throughout this book.

What the numbers show is that those easiest to reach are being reached. For most white Americans—educated, employed, middle and upper class—the cocaine epidemic has peaked. But for the thirteen million (mostly black) children living in poverty, a very dim light shines at the end of the drug tunnel. Many of these children can see nothing but addiction, criminality and violence ahead of them.

The statistics related to the poorest segment of society—children—paint a grim picture of the future. A half million of our children are malnourished. About 100,000 are living on the streets. Two thirds of a million children are abused each year, and almost 40,000 babies die.

For black children, the statistics are especially troubling. Many third world countries have lower infant

Cocaine Use in High Schools

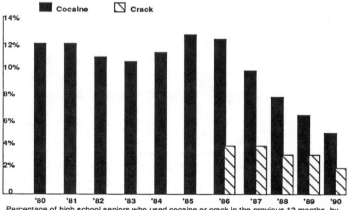

Percentage of high school seniors who used cocaine or crack in the previous 12 months, by year of graduation.

Source: The New York Times

mortality rates than Harlem. Forty-five percent of black children live in poverty. A half million drop out of school each year, and almost that number of black teens give birth.

Prenatal care is almost nonexistent among the poor. The results are premature births, low birth weights, high infant mortality rates and long term problems. Because our government provides less general health care than any other industrialized Western nation, a quarter of a million infants wind up in hospitals fighting for their lives at a cost of $1,000 a day when basic prenatal care might have prevented the problem at a total cost of about $600. We even do an inadequate job of immunizing poor children against preventable diseases like polio, diptheria and tetanus.

And the situation is only getting worse. Between 1979 and 1987, the number of children in poverty increased, while welfare benefits and other assistance to families declined. As the stresses on the poor increase, families become more unstable. In 1960, two thirds of black children lived with both parents. Currently, less than a third do.

For these children—for poor black males, in particular—there is less and less to look forward to. The percentage of black youths entering college has declined sharply in the last decade. Blacks who graduated high school and went to college (a statistic that masks the very high dropout rate black males experience) dropped from 39.8% in 1976 to 30.3% in 1988, while the percentage for whites—even those in low income groups—rose over the same period. The number of black males receiving bachelor degrees declined 12.2%. Unemployment rates continue to be significantly higher for blacks, especially teenage black males, than for whites.

Too often, the alternative to education and employment is drugs, crime and violence. The leading cause of death for black males, ages 20-45, is homicide. One in four black males is under some sort of control within the

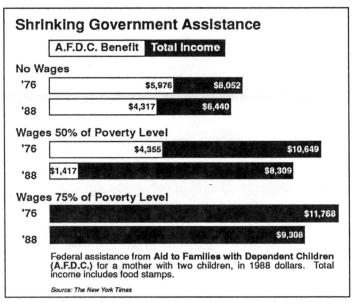

Shrinking Government Assistance

A.F.D.C. Benefit	Total Income

No Wages

'76 — $5,976 / $8,052

'88 — $4,317 / $6,440

Wages 50% of Poverty Level

'76 — $4,355 / $10,649

'88 — $1,417 / $8,309

Wages 75% of Poverty Level

'76 — $11,768

'88 — $9,308

Federal assistance from **Aid to Families with Dependent Children (A.F.D.C.)** for a mother with two children, in 1988 dollars. Total income includes food stamps.

Source: The New York Times

criminal justice system. And although black males constitute only 6% of the total U.S. population, they make up almost half of the U.S. prison population.

We should not be surprised, then, when these excluded, oppressed, angry black kids strike out violently at the society that dominates them.

We prefer to think of street crime, drugs and devastated families as strictly black problems, and to demonize criminals and gang members as monsters. We prefer not to think of these "monsters" as having been created by the racist policies of an oppressive overclass.

But a society that fails to practice social or economic justice is going to spawn monsters. Certainly, crimes must be punished; but crimes must also be understood. A crime may be more than an injustice in itself; it may be a sign of injustice at large. It may be a cry of anger, frustration and protest against a cruel and insensitive society.

If anyone doubts the profound alienation felt by most blacks in America, he or she has only to look at a poll of 484 whites and 408 blacks taken by *The New York Times* and CBS TV news during June 17-20, 1990. Eighty percent of blacks polled believed that white America was singling out black politicians for special investigations and prosecutions. Only a third of whites polled believed that this could be true.

The split was even wider on the issue of drugs, with 50% of blacks agreeing that the government encourages the availability of drugs in poor black neighborhoods. Only 16% of whites agreed with this statement.

Even AIDS feeds conspiratorial fears. Twenty-nine percent of the blacks polled believed that the AIDS virus was deliberately created in a research laboratory by whites in order to infect black people. Only 5% of whites shared this suspicion.

The poll reveals the deep rift between white and black, between overclass and underclass. This rift takes many forms, including the perception among many whites that drug use is declining, while among many blacks it only seems to be getting worse. The level of cocaine use by the overclass is decreasing, but cocaine use by the underclass remains a serious problem, and with it comes terrifying levels of street crime and violence. In the final analysis, the recreational use of drugs by lawyers, stock brokers and other members of the overclass is not going to contribute directly to the record rates of murder and violent crime in our country. It is crime on the streets that terrifies most Americans, and that is what the war on drugs is really all about.

3

Crack Houses, Cracked Homes

A child not yet old enough for kindergarten sits on the floor, staring fixedly at the blaring television, amid rooms in disarray. An air of transience pervades the apartment, as if its occupants are in perennial flight. The baby is as used to white powder, cash, guns, noise and violence as other babies are to bottles, diapers and cribs. Frequently the object of a passing male's casual pique, he learns to fear the angry strangers who snarl viciously and strike out at him. The lack of order in the apartment reflects the incompetence and indifference of a teenage mother whose only purpose is to chase the next high.

Elsewhere, in another apartment, a woman is lying on her stomach on the floor, hands cuffed behind her. An infant cries disconsolately. On a couch sits a male, hands cuffed, speaking into a phone held by an experienced and disillusioned child. The woman screams at the kids not to tell where the drugs are stashed. The cops search the apartment frantically.

And in another precinct, the police plan a raid into a fortified crack house. They worry about dynamiting the steel door. What about the children on the inside?

There are always children.

Children shaped by circumstances that most people never imagine—neglect, beatings, addiction, crime. Children living in heat, cold, filth and disorder. Children who are the frequent targets of mindless violence. Children who quickly learn the uses of such violence. Children who are mere afterthoughts, the byproducts of thoughtless moments of impulse and accommodation.

In homes like these, crack stands at the center of the mother's universe. All else—even the child—is secondary. An enslaving addiction blots everything else out. Even that most enduring and exalted of human qualities—the maternal instinct—is erased by the power of the drug. The refrigerator will be empty, save for some moldy substances whose origins are long forgotten. The furniture will be cheap and in disrepair. Clothes will be soiled and strewn about. Everything in the mother's world will be sacrificed for the relatively inexpensive but powerfully euphoric rush of crack.

The father, of course, cannot be excused from his complicity in this tragedy. He sires children with one woman and then wanders off to prey on the children of other women. Sexual child abuse is a routine occurrence in the culture of crack, as men act out violently and women sell their daughters into prostitution in order to raise desperately needed drug funds.

Violence is routine here. Adults fight over drugs. Dealers punish deadbeats. Domestic arguments are settled with knives and guns.

Addiction and traffic in drugs spark tremendous levels of violence.

Kids age fast in this environment. Toddlers are frequently left on their own for long periods of time. Five-year-olds are forced to cook for and look after their younger siblings. Stories about children falling to their deaths or perishing in fires dot the pages of our city newspapers.

In Oakland, California, a twelve-year-old boy, raised among drug dealers, guns down the man who provides the beepers used by rival drug dealers. (The beepers are used by the drug dealers to communicate with their clients.) In the media, the boy is portrayed as a monster. What the media does not portray are the tears, the grief, the suicide attempts, the beatings and the illnesses the boy experienced growing up in turmoil and uncertainty on the streets.

Much of the drug problem is rooted in issues of economics and class, as the urban poor seek to escape their problems through one of the few kinds of trips available to them: drugs. The poor make up a disproportionate share of the victims of drugs, either as addicts or as innocent—or not so innocent—victims of drug-trafficking violence. Today's shooter is tomorrow's d.o.a.

The most unfortunate casualties of the war on drugs are the children of the poor. Nurtured in violent conditions, crack kids strike out at a world that has been striking out at them. It's hit or be hit, kill or be killed. And I'm only speaking in terms of environmental factors. The genetic implications of maternal crack abuse for children are just as frightening.

Adoption today is a seller's market. For many reasons, including the fact that over 95% of babies born to teenage mothers are being kept and raised by their birth mothers, there are fewer babies available for adoption. Because of this, some intrepid couples have undertaken to adopt or to provide foster care for crack babies. The results have been anything but encouraging.

Children of crack-addicted mothers have been found to have brain damage that causes such dysfunctions as the inability to distinguish right from wrong, to understand cause and effect relationships, to exercise self-control, to express feelings of love and affection, and to concentrate on a task. The symptoms surface gradually over time, their severity determined by the kinds and amounts of drugs ingested by the mother. Crack is a particularly dangerous drug because it affects the mother's body so powerfully and because it is so highly addictive.

Other signs of crack damage in children include spontaneous violent outbursts, dazzling mood swings, refusal to make eye contact, and hyperactivity. Such children cannot be left alone. Nor can they be left to babysitters. Some doctors won't treat them. And schools are finding it difficult, if not impossible, to educate them.

The crack epidemic peaked in the mid-1980s, and inner city schools have been bracing for the first wave of crack babies to enter the educational system in large numbers. Already overtaxed schools will be dealing with large numbers of children with neurological damage and with severe emotional, behavioral and learning dysfunctions. One study has estimated that, out of 375,000 drug-affected births a year in the United States, over 100,000 are crack babies.

Although crack is the central focus of concern, other drugs have also been found to contribute to congenital problems. Among these drugs are cocaine (of which crack is a particularly potent form), heroin, amphetamines, marijuana, alcohol and tobacco. Even one use of cocaine during pregnancy has been found to put a fetus at risk. Chronic use of drugs runs the risk that the woman may damage the fetus before she realizes that she is pregnant.

By the time the child is five, it is hard to distinguish whether the child's behavior has been shaped more by the effects of chemicals ingested by the mother when pregnant or by the brutal conditions of life the child has grown up in. Whichever is the case, dealing with these drug-damaged kids figures to be a daunting and expensive challenge for society at large. These children will require special school programs and specially trained teachers. They may need special health care and psychological treatment. And they threaten to exacerbate the already serious problem of crime in the streets.

The expense of dealing with these kids promises to be astronomical, but failure to deal with them would be even more costly. Studies show that children with low basic skills are nine times as likely as other children to drop out of school, eight times as likely to have a baby outside of marriage and four times as likely to become welfare dependent.

Typical of these drug-damaged children is a four-year-old boy who hit, bit and spat at other children, banged his head on the floor, and had difficulty controlling his movements. He was not toilet trained and didn't speak. The child needed enormous amounts of care and affection. His attention span was one minute, and even after months of patient treatment, he struck out at a visitor.

Over the last quarter century there has been an astonishing shift in the structure of the American family. Twenty-five years ago, the illegimate birth rate among whites was 4%. Now it is 18% and rising. The rate among blacks was 25%. Now it is 63%. Increasing poverty and its attendant evils have contributed mightily to this shift.

Families, usually lone mothers and their babies, make up the fastest growing segment of the enormous and swelling homeless population. These are the circumstances spawning crack babies: a young woman, searching desperately for help, who finds only welfare, pregnancy and illiteracy; a young man, also victimized by unemployment and poverty, conditioned to respond to the woman and her child brutally or indifferently.

This young woman—and others like her—must be taught the harsh realities behind pregnancy and dropping out of school. Too many entertain the naive illusion that a baby and a welfare check constitute a ticket to independence, maturity and one's own place. Too many have been deprived of basic information about human sexuality because of puritanical approaches to sex education. Too many have limited access to contraceptives and birth control information.

The peak in the number of births to teenage mothers occurred in 1972—the year before Roe v. Wade made abortion an option for impoverished women. Even during periods of stringent prohibition, abortions had always been available to middle and upper class women, who could afford to travel where abortions were legal or to maneuver their way around the regulations. Poor women, on the other hand, had neither the means nor the opportunity to procure safe or legal abortions. Something of this cruel double standard still exists today. Manifestations of similar inequities dot the economic landscape.

The growing impoverishment and homelessness of the young pushes them ineluctably toward addiction, violence and crime. Children suffer dislocations of family, friends and place that their fragile psyches cannot support. The incredible contrast between poverty and wealth, visible every day on the streets and in the media, serves as a constant reminder of the injustices and inequities imposed by the overclass on the underclass. These inequities, and the misery they produce, kindles a rage that expresses itself publicly in violent acts of social and self-destruction.

The arrival of the crack babies figures to be just the first appearance of a lost generation that is certain to visit vengeance on its oppressors. The factors contributing to the creation of these "monsters" are varied and complex. They include shifting value systems, the decline of the family and the parlous scarcity of societal benevolence and altruism. Included among the solutions must be adequate housing, economic security, and the adoption of prevention programs that attack the crack problem "upstream" at its sources.

Rather than spending huge sums caring for or trying to control drug-damaged children, ways have to be found to prevent their birth. Young people have to be encouraged to stay in school and achieve strength and independence before taking on adult relationships and responsibilities. Men and women must be counseled in family planning and provided with a full range of birth control options, including safe and inexpensive abortions. Young women must have access to good prenatal care if and when they do become pregnant. Young people have to be given a hope and a vision of the future that supplants welfare dependency. They have to be furnished with a good education and good jobs. What this comes down to is the adoption of government economic policies that strike at the heart of the social inequities that are cracking our country—and our families—in two.

4

A Matter of Addiction

Addiction is characterized by compulsive behavior that you cannot control, that you are driven to engage in, which has a negative and sometimes destructive impact on your work, your relations with your family, and your personal actions. Self-improvement hucksters sometimes say, "Well, why don't we addict ourselves to hard work and exercise and fitness?" But they're not really talking about addiction. You can change your lifestyle, you can impose new disciplines on yourself, you can make it a habit to behave more positively, but that does not mean that you're addicted to anything.

This is not to deny that compulsive behaviors may develop in areas usually thought to be useful, wholesome and good. Compulsiveness can turn even virtue into vice, a product of unreasonable excess. Cleaning house, for example, or dieting or exercising can be taken to counterproductive extremes, and this is the case with an addiction. An addiction, then, is an irresistible compulsion that produces negative consequences.

The signs of addiction are not always clearly visible. There may be few, if any, overt physical symptoms, and what signs there are may be obscured by the addict's impulse to conceal his or her addiction. But eventually addictive behaviors have a way of making themselves apparent.

I once had a friend who was a compulsive gambler. At first, I could not believe that anyone could become enslaved to the habit of wagering—in his case, to betting on horses. But over time I came to understand how real and all-consuming such an addiction could be.

I was friends with the man for about twenty-five years. He apparently was already gambling when I met him, but was just in the beginning stages of his addiction. At that time, he owned an expensive convertible and had a good job selling advertisements over the phone, which didn't require him to work in an office and freed him for track visits all over the east coast. When he would say, "Hey, fellas, let's go to the track!" the invitation would have the zing and zest of great fun: beers, dinner, socializing, careering down the highway with the top down. We looked like the boys of summer out of uniform. The desperation behind this innocent fun didn't begin to surface until later.

The worst alcoholic can't drink much more than about ten dollars worth of booze a day, no matter how thirsty he is. But the compulsive gambler can go, literally, through thousands of dollars in a matter of hours, as I tragically discovered was the case for my friend.

Whenever my friend got his hands on some money, he would go to the local race track. If it was closed, he would go to a track in another state. And he would drive anywhere—and I mean anywhere—just to find a track.

When he couldn't get the money legitimately, he would steal from his wife, from his friends, from anyone. He'd even borrow from loan sharks. Their threats were a continuous shadow over his life. When his mother died, she left a tiny inheritance. He fought with his siblings for money that he wasn't entitled to just so that he could gamble with it. There was nothing outside the track that he considered essential. He never kept enough money for rent, and ended up losing his car. He even did a stint in jail over a blizzard of bad checks.

It was a shameful thing to watch. The gambling dehumanized him, stripped him of all his dignity. He lost his moral compass entirely.

I had a lot of trouble remaining his friend. But I loved him. He had a warm and generous nature. He was an intelligent and able man. Still, I couldn't get past his gambling addiction. It was a sticking point in our lives, and it became a daily issue with us. Early on, he had borrowed $800 from me—about two thirds of my laboriously gathered savings—and never paid me back.

My friend's addiction to gambling wound up killing him. Because he neglected his health, he developed lung and stomach problems. Yet he refused to do anything about them. Gambling was his entire life. That's all he did. Every single day.

Because of my friend's tragedy, I came to a better appreciation of just how resourceful and ingenious a desperate man can be. When obsessed with something, the human animal can be enormously cunning. My friend found endlessly clever ways of satisfying his craving to gamble. He brought more skill and talent to bear on feeding his addiction than I would have thought humanly possible. I think this is true of many addicts. They are accomplished at lying, evading, stealing, cutting corners. Their lives are juggling acts in which they frantically try to keep a number of balls—job, family, friends, money—floating in the air as their addiction slowly grinds them down.

My friend seemed to fall into his addiction by chance, but some people may be genetically predisposed to addictive behaviors. Most of us tend to think of addiction as being a freely made choice rather than a physiological predisposition. Indeed, most treatment programs are built on the notion that an addiction is a behavior learned in response to the need to escape, the desire for pleasure, peer pressure or personal problems. Thus we tell addicts that their behavior is one that they have voluntarily taken up and which they must now voluntarily abandon.

But what if addictions were also caused by irregularities in the brain that made some people more prone to addictive behaviors and, once addicted, less likely to be able to change those behaviors?

Studies of brain chemistry are now beginning to unravel the mysteries of that organ's functioning and to shed light on how the abundance or scarcity of certain chemicals in the brain affects addictive behaviors.

Researchers have identified chemical imbalances in the brain that appear to link genetically transmitted deficiencies with depression, anxiety and intense restlessness, and they are now seeking genetic markers that might serve as early warnings of a possible predisposition to addictive behaviors.

Other researchers are breeding animals with irregularities that cause them to crave drugs. The results are strengthening the scientific claims that at least some addictions are genetically determined. The discovery that over three fourths of alcoholics studied possessed a specific gene is another example of research that points to the possibility of a genetic component to addiction. This discovery, and others like it, hold out the promise of early identification of those with a predilection for addictive behaviors. (There are some ethical and moral questions connected with such early identification, however, including the problem of stigmatization.)

The linking of physiological deficiencies with cravings for drugs encourages the search for new drugs that can satisfy these cravings without resulting in addiction. But it would be imprudent to center all our efforts on searching for safe drugs to treat chemical imbalances, thereby ignoring the environmental and cultural factors that also contribute to addictive behaviors. It is clear that all avenues, physiological and environmental, must be explored and that researchers must be willing to follow any road that leads to a better understanding of addictions and their cures.

While exploring the biological connection, the prudent thing to do, then, is to continue to attack the conditions of life, such as poverty, dysfunctional families, and negative peer pressure that we know help to precipitate drug use. In the complex realities of addiction, it is unwise to concentrate on any single cause or cure. Relying entirely on the hope that scientists will develop a biological risk chart, according to which a magic charm might be prescribed, is bound to result in disappointment, considering the historical complexities and harsh realities that have marked human addictions.

This caveat works two ways. There is no guarantee, for example, that eradicating poverty and racism will end drug abuse. An article in the August 11, 1991 issue of *The New York Times* describes how, in Europe's richest country, an elegant park, the Platzpitz in Zurich, has become a depressing haven for heroin addicts. If such a small, stable, prosperous country as Switzerland can suffer from endemic drug addiction and, consequently, one of the world's highest per capita AIDS rates, then we should not expect a simple panacea for America's complex drug problem.

The theory of a biological predisposition for addiction may answer the question of why some people become addicted the first time they use a drug and others never become addicted despite frequent experimentation. Many addicts report satisfying a deeply felt need with their very first use.

There is dramatic evidence to support the notion that addiction can be prevented in some patients through the administration of medicines that cure or control depression. For example, cocaine has been used by addicts who formerly suffered from depression. These users were drawn to the drug because it eased their depression. Replacing a dangerous, illicit drug like cocaine with safer, clinically administered medicines is an important step forward in the prevention and treatment of addiction.

If chemicals in the brain, or the lack of chemicals in

the brain, and the manner in which nerve cells are connected contribute to or cause hyperactivity, extreme docility and other aberrant mental states, and if some addicts are self-medicating and becoming addicted to illicit drugs because of a physiological need for the relief these chemicals provide, then the search for licit drugs to treat neurobiological irregularities must be vigorously pursued. However, I will repeat my caution that we must also continue to pay attention to those environmental conditions that influence addictive behaviors.

The environmental conditions that shape addiction can be roughly divided into two broad areas: home and society. Primary, both in terms of chronology and influence, is the home. Specifically, it is our parents who have the most to do with what sort of adults we will become. (I use the term "parent" in a general sense, rather than a legal one, to mean any adult principally responsible for raising a child.)

That parents play an important role in their children's lives is obvious. Yet some might take issue with the contention that parents are the major determinants of whether or not their children will become addicted to drugs. But parents do create addictive conditions— through their own addictions, indifference, neglect, abuse, instability, violence, inability to communicate, and ignorance.

It is imperative that parents play a positive and interested role in their children's lives. Good parenting skills are essential. The more competent adults are as parents, the better for all involved. The necessary values are simple to enumerate but difficult to practice. They include the ability to love, to listen to, to care for and to empathize with the child. Any parent, regardless of the economic circumstances, can and should exercise these basic skills.

Parents must also be aware of—and critical of—their own behaviors. Parents are fond of telling their children how to behave, but what kinds of messages are they transmitting through their actions? Actions are what kids take notice of. Actions make a stronger impact than words.

I spent my youth watching my mother go off to work, straining in the cold and the snow and the gloomy darkness. She got up and worked and worked and worked. If she had told me a hundred times that work was noble or that hard work was the only thing that was going to rescue our family, it wouldn't have mattered to me. But the fact that she did, indeed, get up and go to work every day was a simple, eloquent and powerful message. It was a message that will stay with me forever.

Unfortunately, the stable, loving, sober, structured and disciplined home is fast becoming an endangered species. Our traditional value systems are giving way to materialism, self-centeredness and hedonism—values intimately related to addictive behaviors.

Many parents are not only hesitant to scrutinize their own behaviors and to address them directly; they are also hesitant to recognize and deal with the behaviors of their children. Quick to secure professional help when confronted with a physical illness, these parents may cling vainly to the belief that they can handle the addictive behaviors of their children without any outside help. So they try to solve the problem alone, or they ignore it or cover it up and hope it goes away, or they deny a problem even exists. But the worst thing parents can do is to assume that the situation is hopeless—to simply give up on their children.

As a police officer, I have seen parents who were actually relieved to hear of their child's death. You prepare yourself to deliver the tragic notification (always required to be done in person). You knock on the door. The mother answers. You say, "I have terrible news for you. An awful thing has happened. Your son has passed away." And the mother replies, "Well, he gave me so much grief, it's really a relief. I just didn't know what to expect next. I can't say that I'm sorry."

Being raised in a safe and nurturing home improves the odds that a child will turn out drug-free and non-addicted, but it doesn't guarantee it. There are larger societal influences at work, and other factors beyond the parent's immediate control. But parents should never give up. They need to reach out when necessary for professional help; they need to be alert to the signs and symptoms of drug abuse, such as missing money, sudden changes in behavior, and problems at school. Parents need to maintain regular and open channels of communication with their kids. Once an emergency strikes, it's too late to try to unclog those channels. And parents must always remember that curing is a longer and harder process than preventing. There is, finally, no magic formula, no single infallible approach.

If we're emotionally involved with an addict, chances are we're going to do some negative and counterproductive things. Parents have to be very, very wise. Every addict says, "I'll never do it again. I'm gonna stop. I've hit bottom. I'm on my way up. Just help me this one last time." There is a word for people who succumb to these pleas. They're called "enablers." Enablers actually help an addict remain addicted. "Helping" an addict get his alcohol or drugs is harmful to that addict. "Harming" them by not enabling is helpful. Sometimes it's hard to know which is which.

That's why it's important to seek expert advice. There are people who have dedicated their lives to the study of addictive behaviors. The alternative—to believe that you can go it alone, to cover the problem up out of guilt or shame or ignorance—is very dangerous. If we're going to help the addict, we must be prepared for a long and difficult struggle. If we truly care about the person, we'll stick through it.

Of course, there is always the risk of failure in dealing with addiction, and most parents don't like to admit failure—or that they're responsible for their children's problems. Some parents are adept at rationalizing, equivocating, evading the truth. Truth can be a hard thing to confront. The trouble is, you cannot solve any problem unless you first identify and define it. If you refuse to recognize the problem, there is no hope that you will ever be able to solve it.

Denial is a way of avoiding a problem by pretending that it doesn't exist. It is a particular temptation when dealing with the shock and humiliation of drug abuse. Denial, however, won't cause an addiction to disappear. Worse, it gets in the way of curing the problem. An addiction has to be confronted directly. The first step on any road to recovery is the humble acceptance of the burden of guilt. The addict needs to say, "I'm not going to be able to solve this problem until I assume the burden of responsibility." And those who want to help the addict must encourage this acceptance of personal responsibility. We must help addicts to see that they are in the grip of something more powerful than themselves. Until that realization occurs, we're all just shoveling sand against an irresistible tide.

Where can addicts and their families find the help and support they need? From people who've gone through similar experiences, for one. The best treatment programs always include people who have been there, who've experienced the problems of addiction first-hand. These people have the best understanding of the tragedy of addiction in all its dimensions. The real source of the enormous power of Alcoholics Anonymous as a treatment program is the authenticity that comes from the testimony of former users.

I do have some reservations about traditional twelve-step approaches like Alcoholics Anonymous and Gamblers Anonymous, however. One is that although they ask you to confront your addiction, to acknowledge it, to humble yourself and seek help, they don't ask you to delve into what caused the addiction. Curing an addiction requires an awareness of the factors that brought it into being in the first place. The dangers of a relapse are diminished when the addict is made to understand the origins of the problem and is given an opportunity to deal with them.

Alcoholics may say that it was routine social drinking that triggered their alcoholism. Gamblers may lay the blame on repeated wagering. Certainly, repetition plays a part in hooking the user. But many people drink or gamble on a regular basis without ever becoming addicted to either alcohol or gambling. Why is it, then, some people develop addictions?

I think I've figured out why my friend developed his addiction. He was punishing himself for having sexual fantasies about his mother that he could not rid himself of. I often urged him to get therapy and counseling, but his answer to me was that I didn't know what I was talking about. He insisted that his mother was a slut and that he did not respect her. But I knew his mother well. She was just about the most respectable and responsible woman I'd ever met, and being wanton about sex was simply unthinkable. Yet, to his dying day, my friend retained his fantasy, and I believe that his failure to come to terms with the source of his addiction precluded any chance of a cure.

Subconsciously, my friend harbored deep guilt feelings about his fantasies and felt a profound need to punish himself. That is why he went to the track—to lose. So even when he won, he would never think of paying anyone back, including me. His winnings were just more grist for the mill, more money to lose the next time on the track.

There may be many precipitating or predisposing factors for any single addiction, but one factor that encourages addictive behaviors in a very general way in American society today is our insatiable consumerism. We are defined by others, and we define ourselves, as consumers. Yet the "need" to consume is an artificial one. The guilty secret behind America's consumerism is the national genius for marketing that propels the psychic appetite of its citizens.

The ministrations of Madison Avenue make us hungry for satisfaction and desperate for relief. Our brightest and most creative writers, dancers, actors and artists bend their talents daily to convince us to gargle, swallow, annoint, chew, apply or absorb a myriad of substances that are supposed to make us feel better, look better, and function more effectively. Little old ladies swallow handfuls of pills, capsules and tablets without a second thought, even as they call for the death penalty for drug dealers. A society that is so anxious to find pleasure and escape pain through over-the-counter nostrums and prescription drugs should not find the chasm between licit and illicit drugs an unbridgeable one.

Television and its commercials have conditioned us to be avid consumers, even of alcohol and drugs. The power of the medium is enormous. If we intend to win the war on drugs, we're going to have to convince the television and advertising industries to put the genie of drug use back into the bottle. We need to replace the media's slick promotion of legal drugs with a well-organized and sustained mass media campaign to curb drug and alcohol abuse. The elements of such a campaign would replicate traditional advertising techniques: the identification of target audiences; demographic research; information that builds on the audience's existing knowledge; messages that tap the audience's existing motives and desires and that create needs which can be gratified quickly and easily; and the use of media appropriate to the audience and the message. In short, we need to employ the same methods currently being used to seduce us into materialism and hedonism to promote abstinence and responsibility instead.

Changes in behavior take time. Witness the slow evolution in attitudes about cigarette smoking following the Surgeon General's report in 1964. Two things had to happen to change people's attitudes: negative messages about smoking had to be interwoven into television programs and films, and positive images had to be removed. It isn't enough to stick a thirty second anti-smoking commercial between scenes of a television program that shows actors puffing merrily away.

The case could be made that the mass media have turned us into a druggie culture. Alcohol, tobacco and over-the-counter drug ads festoon our airwaves and printed pages. By devoting impressive resources to recent pro bono efforts to combat substance abuse, the advertising industry has tacitly—if not explicity—admitted its responsibility in this matter.

Media heroes set the trends our teenagers adopt. If kids are convinced by the behavior of their heroes that abstention from drugs is cool or hip, they'll abstain from drugs. A generation of young people learned to smoke and drink by watching romantic images of "sophisticated" movie stars smoking and drinking on the screen. Paradoxically, they were also taught the horrors of addiction and drug abuse through the media. Although the anti-drug message made an impact, it was weakened by the contradictory signals that the culture was giving out. To be successful, an anti-drug media campaign has to be broadly encompassing and consistent.

There are many other cultural factors that complicate the problem of addiction, among them a popular music that glorifies drugs, abuse and violence. Demeaning and exploitive lyrics in songs like "Me So Horny" by 2 Live Crew raise the question of whether pop music should be censored. There seems little doubt that referring to women as bitches and graphically describing sexual debasement and assault encourages kids to view women as dehumanized, discardable objects. The lyrics tell young black men that it's okay to brutalize and exploit women—that it's okay to sire children with no sense of responsibility or regret. These misogynistic attitudes feed into the cycles of addiction, violence, racism and poverty I described in earlier chapters. A milieu in which anything is justified in the pursuit of pleasure and in which people feel free to express and act upon any desire or fantasy can only be described as anomic.

And yet we ought not to censor thoughts we hate. We ought to drive them out with disapproval, not legislation. Pop music lyrics are only one example of the many factors that are intertwined with larger issues of class and race, of violence and crime, of drugs and addiction. The problem of negative cultural influences—like the problem of addiction itself—is too multi-faceted, complex and shifting to be solved simply through legislation and enforcement.

Ironically, even though we are winning the battle to educate the American people about addiction and the dangers of drug abuse, we continue to lose the war. How is this possible? The problem is that not everyone is getting the message. Only those who are most "reachable" are being reached; only those most "educable" are being educated; only those most "influence-able" are being influenced. Middle and upper class Americans, in other words, are moving away from certain hard drugs. There are many statistics to support this—statistics which the politicians in Washington have not hesitated to trumpet. But statistics also show that underclass America is more deeply mired in the swamp of drug addiction than ever. This addiction manifests itself in ever-rising levels of violence and crime among the poor, especially the urban poor.

A 1991 survey by the University of Michigan's Institute for Social Research reported that cocaine use by high school seniors had dropped for the fourth consecutive year. For the first time, students reported a decrease in the availability of cocaine and crack on the streets. The number of cocaine users was half of what it was at its high-water mark in 1986.

Yet alcohol consumption remained "staggeringly high." More than 80% of the students reported drinking alcohol within the year and nearly a third admitted that they'd had five or more drinks in one sitting within the past two weeks. Also, about one in five said they smoked daily.

The survey showed that the campaign against cocaine use was proving somewhat successful. But it is significant that the researchers surveyed only high school seniors. Those who had dropped out of school were not included in the survey. And what evidence there was pointed to a significant continuing cocaine problem in the inner city.

The survey also showed that the high school seniors studied were not so much giving up drugs as they were searching for a "safer" high. This is the cycle of seduction, immersion and disillusion I talked about in chapter two: educated and economically mobile users seeking safer routes to pleasure while the underclass remains enslaved by addiction and crime.

The link between addiction and crime is a strong one. If you go to any U.S. prison you will find that the population is disproportionately poor, black, unskilled, and undereducated—and addicted to drugs, alcohol or gambling. It is estimated that 13% of the prison population in America got there because of a gambling problem. If you arrest a thousand street criminals for crimes not directly related to drugs, you will find that two thirds of them have felony drugs in their bodies. By "felony drugs," I mean cocaine, heroin, crack, PCP, angel dust and amphetamines. I'm not including alcohol—the most abused drug in America.

The drug addict's dilemma is different from that of the alcoholic. While an alcoholic may act in a disturbed or uncontrollable fashion, society is generally more tolerant of drunken behavior than it is of what it perceives as the more bizarre aberrancies of drug addicts. Also, illicit drugs tend to be costlier and more difficult to obtain than alcohol. And because the sale, possession and use of illicit drugs are by definition criminal offenses, there is inevitably more crime and violence associated with drug addiction than with alcoholism.

Addicts are not arrested in America for merely being addicts. To be addicted to a drug is not a crime in itself. It is a status. (Status offenses are typically age specific—truancy and underage drinking, for example.) Small-time junkies who get picked up for misdemeanor possession receive relatively mild treatment within the criminal justice system. They usually spend some time locked up when they are first arrested and processed and awaiting trial. And they can expect to spend some time in the county jail. But they rarely go to prison.

Prison time is reserved for more serious drug offenders—those who have committed felonies. Still, there are more than enough felony drug convictions from run-of-the-mill sweeps and roundups to keep the prisons filled to bursting. The U.S. prison population has more than tripled in the last twenty years. In 1970, just over 200,000 people were incarcerated in American prisons. That number rose to 250,000 in 1975, to 300,000 in 1980, to 470,000 in 1985, to 711,000 in 1990, and is expected to reach 1,133,000 by 1995. A significant factor behind this increase is the flood of drug arrests produced by our growing infatuation with low-level street enforcement. These tactics have not reduced levels of addiction or numbers of addicts, but they have reduced the ability of the criminal justice system to function efficiently and effectively.

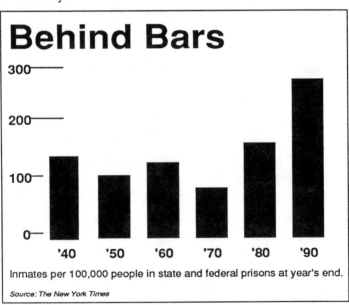

Behind Bars

Inmates per 100,000 people in state and federal prisons at year's end.

Source: The New York Times

Obviously, the easiest, cheapest and most effective way to fight addiction is through prevention. Drug prevention programs are particularly important for the lower classes, who already suffer from inordinate levels of crime, violence and familial dissolution. The upper classes can buffer themselves with money. They can buy what they need: comforts, companionship, education, treatment. That is not to say that the well-off don't have drug problems. They just have more resources for treating, ameliorating or concealing their problems. When an upper class couple divorce, for example, their children do not experience the same economic hardships as those of poorer couples. The children may experience emotional and psychic trauma, and they may become addicted to drugs as a result of that trauma, but they will not experience the same sort of want and deprivation as the poor.

Most importantly—and most logically—drug prevention programs should be directed toward children. The likelihood that any individual will become addicted to drugs is established long before that person reaches adulthood. The earlier in life we attack the problem, the greater the chances for success. In America today we are seeing addictions in younger and younger people. We're even seeing addictions in newborn infants. Over 375,000 babies a year are born addicted to drugs. It is our children who are the most vulnerable casualties of the war on drugs, and it is our children whom we must save if we want to win the war on drugs.

5

Our Children at Risk

One of the things that makes the study of drugs and addiction difficult is the shifting and unstable nature of experimentation and use. At any given time, the popularity of a drug and its population of users are apt to be changing. Over the years, the drugs of choice have included heroin, morphine, cocaine, marijuana, speed, barbiturates, valium, LSD, crack, angel dust, quaaludes, and numerous other natural and designer chemicals. Drugs pass through cycles of ascendancy and decline, with the cycles often overlapping as trend setters take up and abandon drugs, one after another, in a never-ending search for a consequence-free high.

The picture clears somewhat when we narrow our focus to a single group in a single place at a single time. One such snapshot was provided by a 1989 Minnesota poll that surveyed almost 100,000 students, representing two-thirds of the sixth, ninth and twelfth graders in the state. The picture is, to some degree, a skewed one. Minnesota ranks highest of all states in high school graduation rate. It has a relatively small minority population. Its largest city has fewer than 400,000 inhabitants. Its ghettos are idyllic in comparison to the Bronx or Detroit. And its very isolation tends to preserve traditional value sys-

TOP 10 SOURCES OF HAPPINESS
By Gender and Grade

	Females				Males		
Rank[a]	6th Grade	9th Grade	12th Grade	Rank	6th Grade	9th Grade	12th Grade
1	Friends (90%)	Friends (92%)	Friends (91%)	1	Friends (81%)	Making money (81%)	Friends (86%)
2	School (80%)	Buying things (82%)	Buying things (81%)	2	Outdoors (80%)	Friends[b] (81%)	Outdoors (80%)
3	Family (77%)	Music (79%)	Dating (78%)	3	Sports (79%)	Outdoors (77%)	Making money (80%)
4	Buying things (74%)	School (76%)	Doing a good job (76%)	4	Making money (77%)	Sports (74%)	Dating (72%)
5	Outdoors (72%)	Making money (75%)	School (76%)	5	School (74%)	School (70%)	Doing a good job (72%)
6	Making money (72%)	Dating (72%)	Music (74%)	6	Family (73%)	Buying things (70%)	Music (72%)
7	Doing a good job (71%)	Parties (71%)	Making money (72%)	7	Video/Computer games (71%)	Music (66%)	Buying things (72%)
8	Music (69%)	Doing a good job (68%)	Parties (66%)	8	Buying things (70%)	Doing a good job (66%)	Sports (70%)
9	Sports (68%)	Sports (63%)	Outdoors (65%)	9	Doing a good job (70%)	TV/Movies (64%)	Parties (67%)
10	Parties (63%)	Outdoors (63%)	Family (61%)	10	TV/Movies (69%)	Parties (62%)	School (66%)

a In terms of percentage selecting each choice.
b Ranking derived from percentage before rounding.

tems. Still, the survey offers useful insights into the attitudes and behaviors of contemporary youth and provides a meaningful context for the individual case studies I take up in the next chapter.

When we look at how these kids rank the things that make them happy, we see intimations of the declining importance of the family and the growing attraction of materialism. Popularity with peers and the pursuit of pleasure seem to outweigh considerations of service to others or similarly altruistic enterprises. Not coincidentally, peer influence and pleasure seeking are the two main reasons students cite for using drugs.

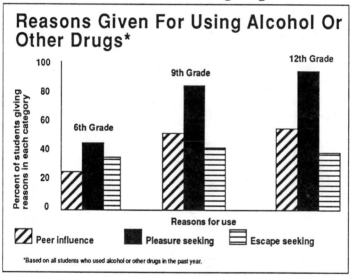

Reasons Given For Using Alcohol Or Other Drugs*

Percent of students giving reasons in each category

Reasons for use

Peer influence   Pleasure seeking   Escape seeking

*Based on all students who used alcohol or other drugs in the past year.

The sources of worry for these kids are many. The world is changing fast for them. Even as the threat of nuclear war declines, the fear of dying from AIDS or contracting sexually transmitted diseases increases. A significant percentage of adolescents report having felt emotional distress of one kind or another in the month previous to the survey. The stresses and pressures on teens have the potential to drive much negative and dysfunctional behavior. About 40% of the students who have used drugs or alcohol in the past year say that they do so to escape worry and distress.

TOP 10 SOURCES OF WORRY
By Gender and Grade

	Females				Males		
Rank[a]	6th Grade	9th Grade	12th Grade	Rank	6th Grade	9th Grade	12th Grade
1	Having friends (58%)	Looks (75%)	School (64%)	1	School (51%)	School (61%)	Job (56%)
2	Looks (57%)	School (69%)	Looks (63%)	2	Having friends (43%)	Having friends[b] (52%)	School (54%)
3	School (57%)	Having friends (68%)	Weight (60%)	3	Dying (42%)	Looks (52%)	Having friends (48%)
4	Dying (48%)	Weight (61%)	Job (59%)	4	Nuclear war (41%)	Job (45%)	Looks (48%)
5	Weight (43%)	Job (46%)	Having friends (54%)	5	Looks (38%)	Nuclear war (29%)	Dying (21%)
6	Job (35%)	Dying (35%)	Pregnancy (33%)	6	Job (38%)	Dying (28%)	Nuclear war (20%)
7	Family fights (35%)	Pregnancy (33%)	Family fights (27%)	7	AIDS (37%)	STDs[*] (23%)	Pregnancy (19%)
8	AIDS (34%)	Family fights (31%)	Dying (27%)	8	Family poverty (29%)	AIDS (22%)	Weight (17%)
9	Nuclear war (32%)	Nuclear war (28%)	Nuclear way (21%)	9	Family fights (29%)	Weight (19%)	STDs[*] (17%)
10	Family poverty (27%)	STDs[*] (19%)	STDs[*] (14%)	10	STDs[*] (25%)	Family fights (18%)	AIDS (15%)

a In terms of percentage selecting each choice.
b Ranking derived from percentage before rounding.
* Sexually transmitted diseases.

EMOTIONAL DISTRESS PAST MONTH					
	Females			Males		
	6th Grade %	9th Grade %	12th Grade %	6th Grade %	9th Grade %	12th Grade %
Feel fresh and rested (never or rarely)	21	36	40	23	31	33
Tired or burned out (all or most of the time)	16	34	43	15	24	30
Mood bad or up and down	56	64	65	50	47	48
Stress or pressure (quite a bit or almost more than I could take)	16	33	48	18	24	35
Sad (all or most of the time)	11	17	14	6	6	6
Discouraged or hopeless (extremely so or quite a bit)	12	20	16	12	12	11
Nervous, worried or upset (all or most of the time)	13	23	22	10	11	12
Satisfied with personal life (somewhat or very dissatisfied)	17	34	28	12	21	22

Breaking the study down by sex reveals the persistence of stereotypical gender roles. Females worry more about their looks, weight and health than do males. Males worry more about material success. Males value making money; females, spending it.

PERCEPTIONS OF GENERAL HEALTH AND WEIGHT						
	Females			Males		
	6th Grade %	9th Grade %	12th Grade %	6th Grade %	9th Grade %	12th Grade %
RATINGS OF GENERAL HEALTH						
Excellent	31	28	30	41	45	49
Good	59	62	62	51	48	47
Fair or poor	10	10	8	8	7	5
HEALTH RELATED TO OTHERS YOUR AGE						
Healthier	14	18	19	21	33	38
About the same	82	76	76	75	63	59
Not as healthy	4	6	6	4	4	3
PERCEPTION OF WEIGHT						
Underweight	11	7	5	15	19	22
About right	63	51	49	67	64	62
Overweight	26	42	46	18	18	16

PHYSICAL VIOLENCE AND SEXUAL ABUSE

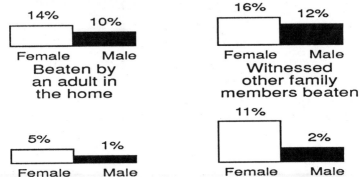

14%   10%
Female   Male
Beaten by an adult in the home

16%   12%
Female   Male
Witnessed other family members beaten

5%   1%
Female   Male
Sexually abused by a family member

11%   2%
Female   Male
Sexually abused outside the family*

*Excluding forced sexual contact by a date or friend

LOW SELF-ESTEEM						
	Females			Males		
	6th Grade %	9th Grade %	12th Grade %	6th Grade %	9th Grade %	12th Grade %
I usually feel good about myself. . . . . . . (Disagree)	13	24	20	10	12	11
I am able to do things as well as most other people . . . .(Disagree)	10	13	10	10	8	6
On the whole I'm satisfied with myself . (Disagree)	13	24	19	10	11	10
I do not have much to be proud of . . . . . . (Agree)	18	24	18	16	16	15
Sometimes I think I'm no good . . . .(Agree)	33	43	32	27	24	20
I feel that I can't do anything right . . . . (Agree)	21	26	18	16	15	10
I feel that my life is not useful . . . .(Agree)	15	22	14	13	14	11

More disturbing, however, is the continuing, often violent, victimization of females in this culture. A significantly greater number of females than males report that they have been physically or sexually abused at least once in their lives. More than one in seven females have been beaten by an adult in the home, and sixteen percent have been sexually abused. No wonder, then, that females suffer from greater emotional distress and experience lower self-esteem than do males.

RELIGIOUS INVOLVEMENT	6th Grade %	9th Grade %	12th Grade %
FREQUENCY OF RELIGIOUS SERVICE ATTENDANCE			
Weekly	56	53	34
Monthly	14	17	21
Rarely	20	20	32
Never	10	11	12
IMPORTANCE OF RELIGION IN YOUR LIFE			
Very Important	24	18	18
Pretty Important	38	37	35
A Little Important	28	32	33
Not Important	10	13	15

RISK-TAKING
"Get a kick out of dangerous things"

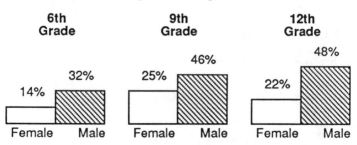

6th Grade	9th Grade	12th Grade
Female 14% / Male 32%	Female 25% / Male 46%	Female 22% / Male 48%

Use In The Past Year

	6th Grade %	9th Grade %	12th Grade %
Alcohol	8	47	76
Tobacco	6	28	41
Marijuana	*	9	18
Speed or Amphetamines	*	5	6
Cocaine (powder or crack)	*	2	3
Inhalants (glue, paint, etc.)	2	4	2
Sedatives	*	2	1
Other Illegal Drugs	*	3	3
Other People's Prescriptions Drugs	2	4	3
Steroids	*	1	1

*less than 1%

The survey reveals a significant decline in religious involvement as the young people grow older. Conversely, the tendency of young people to take risks increases with age. Perceptions of emotional distress also tend to increase with age.

It's not surprising, given these changes in values and self-perception, that all types of drug and alcohol use increase with age, including occasional use, regular (at

Regular Use In The Past Year**

	6th Grade %	9th Grade %	12th Grade %
Alcohol	3	27	55
Tobacco	3	20	31
Marijuana	*	5	10
Speed or Amphetamines	*	2	3
Cocaine (powder or crack)	*	*	1
Inhalants (glue, paint, etc.)	*	2	*
Sedatives	*	1	*
Other Illegal Drugs	*	2	1
Other People's Prescriptions Drugs	1	2	*
Steroids	*	*	*

*less than 1%
**Regular use is defined as at least monthly use of the substance

Prevalence Of Problem Use*

☐ Female ■ Male

6th Grade **9th Grade** **12th Grade**

17% 23%

9% 9%

1% 1%

*Problem use is defined as at least monthly use of alcohol or drugs
with three or more adverse consequences of use.

least monthly) use and problem use (regular use that
results in at least three adverse consequences). The
prevalence of consequences from drug and alcohol use
also increases with age.

The survey reveals a strong connection between
difficulty with reading and a dislike for school, which, in
turn, is linked with problem alcohol and drug use.

BELIEF THAT OTHER PEOPLE CARE ABOUT YOU

NUMBER RESPONDING "VERY MUCH" & "QUITE A BIT"	6th Grade %	9th Grade %	12th Grade %
Adults care about you	80	70	71
School people care about you	53	41	42
Parents care about you	94	88	89
Friends care about you	72	73	77
Church leaders care about you	64	52	44
Family cares about your feelings	78	65	67
Family understands you	65	44	45
Family has fun together	67	45	40
Family respects your privacy	64	52	58

Reading problems begin early in a student's life. Indeed, it seems that every time we scrutinize a problem, our attention is drawn upstream. When kids start out behind their peers—even in kindergarten—they begin to develop negative attitudes about learning and school. Kindergarten problems point to the importance of pre-

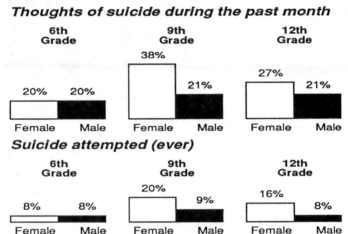

SUICIDAL BEHAVIOR
Thoughts of suicide during the past month

	6th Grade	9th Grade	12th Grade
Female	20%	38%	27%
Male	20%	21%	21%

Suicide attempted (ever)

	6th Grade	9th Grade	12th Grade
Female	8%	20%	16%
Male	8%	9%	8%

school programs like Head Start. Success in preschool, in turn, is affected by such upstream factors as birth weight and early nurturing. Finally we are led back to the importance of prenatal care and the personal health habits of the mother.

The epidemic of teenage suicide in this country is also reflected in the survey. Approximately 12% of the students reported that they had attempted suicide at least once in their lives. A phenomenal 25% reported having considered suicide in the month preceding the survey. Low self-esteem, high levels of emotional distress, and anti-social behaviors correlate strongly with the rate of attempted suicides, as do physical and sexual abuse and

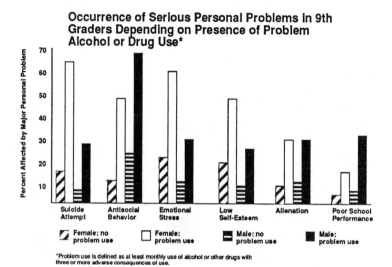

Occurrence of Serious Personal Problems in 9th Graders Depending on Presence of Problem Alcohol or Drug Use*

*Problem use is defined as at least monthly use of alcohol or other drugs with three or more adverse consequences of use.

problem use of alcohol and drugs in families. Again, all of these factors, including suicide attempts, correlate strongly with problem alcohol and drug use by adolescents.

Studies have repeatedly shown that American females have sex as early and as often as their European counterparts. Still, more than half of all American teenagers are sexually active, and the age of first intercourse is getting lower and lower. Also, American teenagers produce many more babies, and they are much more likely to keep them. This fact points to the need for better sex education and greater availability of contraceptives. Our puritanical views about sex result in too many abortions that could have been prevented and too many births that should have been prevented.

That parents and teachers are failing to educate young people about sex and sexual responsibility is indicated by the sources of sex information cited by the students in the survey. Teenagers get most of their

SEXUAL BEHAVIOR

	9th Grade	12th Grade
Has had sexual intercourse	Female 22% Male 35%	Female 60% Male 62%
If sexually active, always uses birth control	Female 37% Male 37%	Female 59% Male 49%
If sexually active, always uses condoms	Female 41% Male 46%	Female 25% Male 32%

information about sex from their peers and the popular media—sources that are likely to provide distorted or inaccurate information. Ignorance, misplaced religious convictions and inflexible moral codes are unquestionably contributing to the crisis of teenage pregnancy and motherhood.

The survey also reinforces the importance of the family in relation to alcohol and drug use. Over 70% of the problem users in the survey report the existence of serious family problems. This statistic is especially alarming in light of the fact that nearly one in four students report alcohol and drug problems in their families. Clearly, the traditional American family, as an institution, is in very serious trouble.

86

FAMILY ALCOHOL AND DRUG PROBLEMS

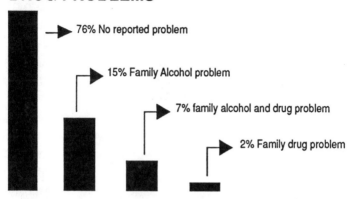

76% No reported problem

15% Family Alcohol problem

7% family alcohol and drug problem

2% Family drug problem

The survey identifies alcohol and tobacco as the most commonly used drugs. This is not surprising given the demographics of the students surveyed. Still, though the consequences of licit drug use are very different from those of illicit drug use, we should not minimize the dangers of alcohol and tobacco abuse. The thousand people a day killed by tobacco and the third of a thousand killed by alcohol vastly outnumber the fifteen per day who die from heroin, cocaine and other illicit drugs.

In another recent survey—this one sponsored by the Lutheran Brotherhood—5,300 letters written to U.S. Congressmen by seventh and eighth grade students were analyzed, and the top seven concerns of these adolescents were determined to be: drug abuse (25%); sex and pregnancy issues (17%); environmental issues (10%); crime, including gang violence, gun control and capital punishment (7%); education (5%); child abuse (5%); and suicide (5%). Other concerns included homelessness, satanism, drunk driving, college funding, social security and Medicare, sexism, cruelty to animals, eating disorders, runaways, divorce, and television.

Obviously, today's young people have much more on their minds than merely running in the halls or chewing gum—and for good reason. The social health index, computed by the Children's Defense Fund, measures rates of infant mortality, child abuse, children living in poverty, teen suicide, drug abuse and dropping out of school. According to the index, four of these six categories have worsened in the last twenty years, with child abuse increasing the most. Increased reports of child abuse may be at least partly due to heightened awareness and improved reporting, but the statistics nevertheless indicate a shocking decline in the care and welfare of our children, especially poor children. Teenage suicide has doubled in the last two decades. The number of children living in poverty has risen 25%. One in five children now lives in poverty. An estimated 100,000 children go to sleep homeless every night, and five times that number suffer from malnutrition and undernourishment. A million teenage girls become pregnant each year, and almost one fourth of all students fail to complete high school. More and more children are being cared for by strangers—or simply left to their own devices—as families fall apart or parents are forced to work outside the home. These trends largely affect the underclass, and do so with particular force.

Sometimes in the crush of statistics we lose sight of the flesh and blood actors in this grim human drama. The painful but heroic stories of kids who must deal directly and routinely with a world of drugs, poverty and family dysfunction can help us see the reality behind the abstractions of data. In the next chapter, I talk one-on-

one with eighteen kids who have had to face such a world head on. They tell their stories straight, in their own words, and in the process they bring the tragedy of childhood drug addiction to life.

6

The Kids*

There is an awful sameness about the
lives of institutionalized adolescent addicts.   Locked up, forced to undergo
treatment, counting the hours to the ap-
pointed moment of release, they are im-
prisoned by addictions that prod, pry and
tempt their psyches every hour of every
day.   Captivated by inner voices that
continually attempt to seduce them back
into old habits, they must endure recurring
thirsts and hungers that they can never
satisfy, not even once.

And yet there is a wonderful beauty in
their humility and in the simple way they
accept their fate.   Although they don't
always express it directly, their talk is
laced with personal regret and warnings
for others: don't do it, resist, don't chain
yourself to this rock. These kids know that
people never intend to get hooked on

drugs, that most people think it can't happen to them—and they know the folly of such hubris.

Here are the stories of a few of these kids.

Seth

Seth glowers. His looks are menacing, provoking feelings of defensiveness and bellicosity in those who meet him. At seventeen, he has been in more hot water than most people get into in a lifetime.

Seth got drunk for the first time at age twelve, drinking four beers in the basement of a friend's house. Fifteen other underage kids were also partying there that day.

That same year Seth tried pot in a cornfield with two other friends. He had picked the roaches (marijuana butts) out of the ashtray of his older brother's pickup truck.

Seth used drugs only occasionally until age fifteen, when he began to drink and smoke pot on a daily basis. He also began to sell drugs in order to support his habit. In very little time he was dealing a pound of marijuana a week.

Soon the consequences of his illicit drug use began to increase. ("Consequences" is a word that recurs often in these kids' stories.) Seth was kicked out of school in the ninth grade for fighting. The next year he was expelled for doing drugs. Once, Seth came home drunk and fought with his father. His father picked up a shovel and swung at Seth, missed, fell, and broke his nose. After the police were called, Seth was charged with assault and forced into treatment for chemical dependency. Seth's brief time in jail proved an eye-opening experience.

"I was scared," Seth recalls. "I almost got into a couple of fights, but the staff broke us up. The other kids were doing gross stuff." (Such euphemisms as "gross stuff" conceal the true hideousness of incarceration: routine sexual and physical assaults and other atrocities.)

Beneath his tough guy exterior, Seth is a pleasant kid. He lives with his biological parents, an older brother and a grandmother. Both of Seth's parents work, his father as a teacher and his mother as a secretary. His dad used to go regularly to a bar to drink but has stopped. His mother doesn't drink at all. His older brother smokes pot and drinks. Seth thinks that his brother is chemically dependent but that he gets away with it because the dependency doesn't lead to any trouble.

"I get in trouble because I can't control it," says Seth. "I'm violent as hell when I get drunk. The adrenaline starts flowing. I would steal, break apartment windows, smash car windows. One time a driver was tailgating us and we threw bottles at him."

Seth is on medication for an attention deficit disorder that makes him impulsive.

"I don't think before I act," Seth says.

Seth feels a lot of pent-up anger. Drugs help to release some of that anger, although not constructively. It's possible that Seth's frustrations have biological roots and that his addiction constitutes a rough form of self-medication.

How did Seth get hooked on drugs?

"It just started happening," Seth recalls. "Partying. There were no problems. I liked it. It made me feel good."

Seth has been in treatment for four weeks. This is his

first time, and he hopes to get out in ten days. He wants to start a new life, join AA, get his G.E.D., work in his brother's body shop and get married in about a year and a half.

Is Seth chemically dependent?

"Yes," he says. "I liked smoking pot."

Jason

Jason is only fifteen years old, but already he's been through chemical dependency treatment in over twenty-five different institutions. Like Seth, his defiant swagger and permanent sneer buy him more trouble than he probably realizes. He is laconic to the point of sullenness, and it takes considerable probing to uncover the nice young man behind the tough facade.

Jason's mother and father are both alcoholics, although his mother has now quit drinking. Two of his siblings, a fourteen-year-old sister and a twelve-year-old brother, are also chemically dependent.

Jason first got high at the age of five when his father gave him some beer to drink. When he was ten, he began to sneak beers out of the refrigerator and drink on the sly. He still feels guilty about giving his eight-year-old sister some beer "to experiment."

After the seventh grade, Jason decided to drop out of school. Instead of finding a legitimate job, he learned how to hotwire cars, stole thirty of them in all, and traded the cars for dope.

"My mom found drugs and sent me to treatment," Jason explains. "After I got out, she found more drugs. Then I went to treatment again.

"I was taken advantage of—sexually—and abused

six or seven times. It would happen at parties when I was high. I raped someone. I'm ashamed of it and feel guilty."

Jason hit bottom when a guy he had cheated in a drug deal threatened to hunt him down and kill him.

"I didn't know where to turn," says Jason. "He tried to run me over. Another time he came up behind me on a beach and tried to drown me."

Jason fled to a friend's house in another town and stayed a week. The he heard that the guy who was after him was in jail, so he returned home.

Jason has been in treatment for a month. He has another week to go before he is to be released. Then he must go to a halfway house, and after that, a foster home.

Is Jason chemically dependent?

"Yes," he says. When he was using, he preferred acid, which he placed in his mouth and sucked. He also used alcohol, pot, coke, speed, crack, inhalants, and hallucinogenic mushrooms.

How did he get hooked on drugs?

"I liked it," Jason says. "Everyone else does it."

Whom does he blame for his drug problem?

"Myself," he says—although later he will also blame his father.

Who started him on drugs?

"Dad," says Jason.

Who kept him using?

"Me," he replies, though others share the blame—in this case, his friends.

Jason doesn't want to return home. He feels neglected there. He is hopeful that his treatment will work this time, and yet he is scared that he might never be able to stop. Jason is not convinced that the staff cares much about him.

How does he feel about himself?

"Not too good, but better." He hates being locked up. He's looking at himself more, at the things he can do with his life, but he doesn't feel that he has many options. He is vague about getting an education, finding a career. He mentions enrolling in a college of music, playing the guitar, but it all seems misty and uncertain. Whatever the future holds, Jason hopes that drugs will not be included.

Can he stay sober?

"It won't be easy," he says. "My old friends are a problem. I need to meet new people."

Sally

Sally is sixteen years old. She has been in treatment twenty days and has two more weeks to go. Her parents are divorced, and she lives with her mother, a bakery manager, and an eighteen-year-old brother who is addicted to alcohol and marijuana. Her father, an auto mechanic, is drug-free. Though he lives nearby, "he was not there for my brother or me all our lives," says Sally.

"I first got high at age twelve," she says, "on a bottle of creme de menthe a friend stole from her parents. I drank half the bottle and threw up. I did it out of curiosity and thought it was cool. It was weird."

After that, Sally got high on a regular basis, smoking marijuana that she bought from her brother or his friends. She would smoke anywhere—in the park, at the movies, in the yard. She used with friends she had grown up with.

"I was medicating my feelings," she says. "I'd fight with my mom and then get high."

When Sally was in the ninth grade, her father

effectively gave up on her and her brother.

"He realized my brother was using and got angry," Sally says. "He considered us dead."

That summer, Sally began to use pot and alcohol more heavily, and that Christmas she dropped out of school.

Her drug habit worsening, Sally took a job in a bakery selling donuts. Soon, she was stealing money from the till. When she took $200, the shortage was noticed, and even though it was her uncle's store, he pressed charges against her.

"Mom was glad he did," she says, "and I was, too—later. It brought a consequence."

One day, Sally downed twenty-two beers in a seven hour period. She couldn't stand up. Her head was spinning. She threw up. The police took her to the medical center and then to the detoxification center.

"It was scary," she recalls. "I was alone. Mom didn't help."

Sally was sinking low. She hit rock bottom when her boyfriend beat her up for refusing him sex. In a drunken fury, he nearly drowned her. She couldn't remember anything for three days afterwards.

Sally's mom had long suspected that her daughter had a drug problem. When she found marijuana in Sally's coat pocket, she brought her daughter to the treatment center.

"I was angry at first and denied everything," says Sally. "I was convinced I didn't have a problem. But now I'm glad I'm here. I don't want to waste my life. Drugs wrecked my life. I dropped school and couldn't get a decent job. I was abusive towards my mother and brother. I was selfish and self-centered and didn't like myself. I tried suicide five or six times in eighth grade. I slit my wrists and bandaged them. I was too scared to tell anyone. My mom didn't find out, but it was an attention-getter with friends."

Sally wants to return to school, get her diploma and join the navy.

Is Sally chemically dependent?

"I'm an addict—an alcoholic," she says.

Drug preferences?

"Alcohol—beer or Windsor," she replies. "Marijuana, too."

Why did she use these drugs?

"It was fun," she says. "I liked the feeling of living life on the edge."

Has the treatment helped her?

"People care about me," she says. "My family is helping. I'm talking about feelings and things that happened. I hated myself and was self-destructive. Now I'm sober and like myself a lot more, but I have a long way to go."

Amanda

With her wholesome girl-next-door looks, sixteen-year-old Amanda looks like she ought to be a member of her high school cheerleading team. There is no outward sign of the chemical addiction that took her from alcohol ("anything in hard liquor, but vodka was my drug of choice") to speed ("I had taken ten pills at a youth night dance and wound up shaking and throwing up on the bathroom floor and couldn't hold anything down for four days") to pot ("I didn't like paying for it—too expensive and not a high I liked") to acid ("I had my license for two weeks when I drove to a pool hall. A male friend dared me to suck acid. I was flipping out. The trees were melting into the road. Things were floating in the room. I took three hits. It lasted fourteen hours. I was a mess. I couldn't sleep.")

Amanda overdid everything. Excess was her style. Yet she hated and feared the loss of control that alcohol and other drugs caused.

Amanda comes from what appears to be a "normal" home, occupied by her biological parents and an older brother. Both parents work. Dad has a couple of beers now and then, but Mom doesn't drink at all. Her brother has no drug problems, though he did leave home for several weeks when he was sixteen, after fighting with his father. However, things improved for him dramatically on his return home even as they seemed to get worse for Amanda.

Up until the ninth grade, Amanda says she was "a normal kid." She made good grades, was on the track team, and enjoyed horseback riding. Then her male cousin, who had been abandoned by his alcoholic mother, moved into the house.

"He fit in with the users," Amanda says. "I befriended his friends and dropped mine. They were more fun. They did spontaneous stuff."

On her birthday that year, Amanda and a girlfriend had planned to have breakfast before school. On the way to the breakfast place, they ran into some of their schoolmates who were drinking. Amanda and her friend were unable to resist the entreaties of their schoolmates to join in, and the result was that the two girls arrived at school drunk. Amanda got sick and vomited. She was taken to the school nurse, given a five-day suspension, and was required to go through an alcohol assessment at a hospital before being allowed back in school.

This was not the first time that Amanda had gotten drunk. In the second grade, at an anniversary party for a relative, her brother, who was four years older than her, put a beer keg nozzle in her mouth and dared her to see how much she could drink. But she had not gotten drunk since then. After the incident on the morning of her birthday, however, she began to drink regularly.

"I used every other weekend, but I'd do a lot more alcohol than a person could handle," Amanda says. "I'd throw up and drink some more. I used a lot of pot, too."

Amanda's parents worked to keep her sober. They'd ground her, and she'd get mad and try to get back at them. Once her mother found two bottles that Amanda had hidden and poured them out.

"I fought with her and threw things," Amanda recalls. "I felt it was my life going down the drain."

Amanda spent five days in an adolescent crisis unit and ten days in a multi-diagnostic facility for patients who are suicidal or violent. She went through the 12-step Alcoholics Anonymous program but found it mechanical and never really committed to it.

"I want to be straight, but it's going to be hard," Amanda says. "All kinds of consequences hit me. Sexual, too. I'd see a movie with actors drinking, and I'd want to drink. I blame myself, no one else."

Amanda has been in her present treatment program one month. She has ten more days to go. She likes this program because the staff is caring and "you get to really look at yourself."

Amanda is open, realistic, hopeful. She's walked a

dark, painful, tortuous path and isn't quite sure how she got to where she is now. She knows she still faces a tough road ahead, but she also knows that to wander off that road again would make her life even tougher.

Sylvia

At seventeen years old, Sylvia has lived in foster homes most of her life, shunted from place to place, sometimes ignored, sometimes abused. Her father is an unemployed alcoholic who spends most of his time playing cards with his cronies. Her mother works long hours at a restaurant, and although she and her mother don't live far apart, they seldom visit except over the phone. Sylvia likes her current foster parents because they make her feel so at home.

Sylvia has had a tough life. She had her first drink when she was just five years old.

"Dad gave us cognac to taste," she remembers. "It burned. I almost threw up. He was trying to get us to dislike it."

Sylvia started sneaking alcohol out of a bottle at age seven—"because of my dad. It didn't seem to hurt him." But it did make her sick.

Her parents, she says, gave her money instead of attention, so she spent the money—and got attention— by drinking with her friends. Usually, the friends were older than her and had their own money to spend as well.

"I liked getting drunk," she says. "I'd be laughing and making jokes. I didn't care what happened. We'd trash cars and have drinking games and sit around or drive."

Sylvia was sexually molested by a friend of the family

when she was seven years old. She still sees the man around. He always eyes her suspiciously, as if afraid she'll tell. She was raped by another man at age fifteen. Her mother and father "got on her" over it. Her brother called her a prostitute. "It wasn't true," she says.

Lonely and depressed, Sylvia attempted suicide three times: twice by overdosing on codeine and once by slashing her wrists.

"I didn't care about myself," she says. "I wasn't worth anything."

There were other consequences of her drug use besides suicide and depression.

"I burned the house down because I was careless with cigarettes," she says. "That's how I wound up on probation and in foster care. My parents neglected me. I messed up my senior year in school. I haven't drunk that much this year." She mentions that the treatment she's getting may be working.

Sylvia was evaluated and entered treatment for chemical dependency in May, 1990. Before she stopped using, her drug of choice was hard liquor, although she drank beer and wine coolers, too. "I've done pot, codeine, and laced my joints with hash oil," she says.

Is Sylvia chemically dependent?

"I'm an alcoholic," she replies.

Whom does she blame for her drug problem?

"My dad." She hesitates. "Myself now. I used to blame him. Dad made it seem okay. Doctors told him to stop, but he hasn't. Now he's dying of cancer. He's lost a lot of jobs."

"I'm feeling better about myself now. I'm having my best year. Being sent away helped me. People care about me. I care about myself."

Cheryl

Cheryl is a small, slim young woman, sweetly direct and unaffected. Her father's itinerant career took her from her native California to Minnesota, then back to California.

When Cheryl was six, her mother went on vacation—and never returned. In fact, she was running away from an alcoholic husband who beat her. But she left behind two daughters: Cheryl and Cheryl's three-year-old sister. Cheryl is very explicit about this episode, even though she can't recall anything in her life before it. The parting scene is especially vivid in her memory. "I can still see my mother saying she'd be back in a couple of weeks," says Cheryl.

A life of confusion and wandering followed as Cheryl's father lost jobs, drifted and drank. The two little girls were forced to endure a nightmare of alcoholism, economic instability, abuse and uncertainty.

Cheryl sought to escape her situation through drugs: alcohol, pot, speed and acid. The drugs made her feel better—at least for the moment. At age fifteen, however, her addiction got out of hand, and Cheryl was sent to a treatment center in Minneapolis. Cheryl's mother was also living in Minneapolis at this time, trying to cope with her own instability and the guilt she felt for deserting her daughters. After forty-six days of treatment, Cheryl went to live with her mother and her mother's boyfriend.

Cheryl blames herself for the chaos in her life. Her directness and honesty help her to admit things that for many people would be humiliating and degrading. She confronts her past behaviors frankly because she knows

103

that is the only way to avoid a relapse. Cheryl's biggest dream is to stay sober—today. And to stay sober, she must continue to examine herself and her behavior unflinchingly.

Randy

Sixteen-year-old Randy has been in and out of chemical treatment centers and juvenile detention centers. He entered his current treatment program six weeks ago and is scheduled to get out in two weeks. He then plans to return to the home he shares with his natural father and mother—a situation that makes him something of a rarity among his drug using peers. And yet Randy's home life has been anything but idyllic.

"My father was an alcoholic," he says. "He used to come home high all the time. Mom and Dad have changed a lot. Mom hit me a lot when I was a kid." Randy's mother beat him with a belt. He remembers having welts all over his legs.

Driven by his own addiction, Randy stole, fought, got expelled from school, lost his driver's license—and worried about the mysterious nervous cravings that wouldn't let him rest. When Randy was using, his drug of choice was pot, but he would use alcohol if that was all he could get. Sometimes he sniffed glue. Acid, however, made him "edgy."

"Pot relaxed me," he says. "It put me in another state of mind. I didn't care. I'd do anything without worrying about it."

Why did he stop using?

"I was getting into fights with Ma," he replies. "I got kicked out of school for drinking. I had fights with kids in school. I was always ready to fight if I was high. Nothing mattered."

Who's to blame for his drug problem?

"Myself," he says. "There was a lot of peer pressure. Everybody was into it. It was so much fun."

Randy wants to return to his home and to his school, but not to his using friends or to his old habits. He says he's taking things "one day at a time." The weekly drug tests encourage him to stay clean. Randy doesn't believe that you can just say "no" to drugs unless you're given good reasons not to use—like the drug tests.

"I had to go through pain to stop," he says. "I went through hell. And I lost the trust of my family."

Randy wears a cast on his wrist. He broke it in anger, slamming the wall after an unhappy telephone conversation with his mother.

The pain continues.

Barbara

Seventeen-year-old Barbara remembers the first time she got drunk. It was at a cousin's wedding reception when she was fourteen. Another cousin, she learned later, had planned to get her loaded on beer.

Barbara comes from a midwestern state hundreds of miles from Minnesota. She has been in evaluation and treatment for a month. She is due to get out in another month.

"I wound up in the hospital seven weeks ago for chemical dependency," she says. "I'd been to AA a year ago for the hell of it. I knew I didn't have a problem. I told my social worker six months ago that I did acid. I told Mom, too. They had me assessed. I had trouble my first time in treatment because I didn't recognize my problem—yet I couldn't stay straight. This time, I entered treatment voluntarily. Now I believe it when they tell me I'm in the mid to late stages of chemical dependency. I felt guilty about taking all this crap, so I made myself throw up. My drug of choice was pot. I'd pick acid over beer."

When she took acid, Barbara reported seeing color trails when she moved her hand across her field of vision. Things appeared to melt. There were skeletons all over the floor. She describes these experiences as "weird and scary." Ashes, she says, were jumping out of ashtrays and bugs were "trying to crawl all over me and kill me." "I kicked a pile of dirt and saw worms crawling out," she adds. "I saw them all over me."

Barbara lives with her divorced mother and a fifteen-year-old brother.

"I met with my father in Cincinnati a year ago," she says. He's a firefighter—and an alcholic. But he goes to AA. He left us eight years ago."

When asked why she wants to quit drugs, Barbara cites "the consequences," her fights with her mom and the loss of family trust. "I need my brother's respect," she says.

Whom does she blame for her drug problem?

"Nobody," she replies. "I wanted to try it. It was fun on weekends. I did it with my cousin and friends." She explains that she alone is responsible for her predicament. "I manipulated others to get what I wanted."

Barbara intends to return to her mother's house—"hopefully." (That word "hopefully" qualifies many of these kids' plans for the future.) After she gets out, she will have to attend AA meetings and see a counselor regularly. There will be three weeks of school left, and she would like to finish her junior year if it is at all possible.

"My mom trusted me," she says. "She went to England and left me in charge of the house. I betrayed her trust—and my friends used me. There were people over every single day. I tried to clean things up, but there were signs. My mom was hurt and mad. I felt guilty."

Now Barbara is slowly trying to regain her family's trust. "Mom's happy for me," she says. "She's proud of me. I'm getting help."

Though she is resentful of the confinement and discipline of the treatment program, Barbara finds it helpful because it forces her to confront her past behaviors. She is finding out whom she hurt, and she's learning to show her feelings. She senses, with some relief, that she is losing her power to manipulate her mother. She's glad that she told her social worker that she was using.

Will she make it?

"I think so," she replies.

Why did she use?

"I wanted to feel something," she says. "I took medicine from the cabinet when I realized two beers weren't enough. I'm glad I have sober friends, and that I can do sober things with them. But my best friend uses. It'll kill us not to see each other."

Barbara is worried about her friend. They had been writing every day, but now Barbara hasn't heard anything for a week. The last she heard, her friend was depressed about a guy and doing poorly in school. Her friend may still be doing acid.

"I love to get high on acid," Barbara says. "I'd do a

trip right now—except for the consequences."

Stan

Stan is generally a sweet, gentle and caring kid, but he has a history of acting out violently when provoked—a latter-day Billy Budd. Stan has been in his current treatment program for only ten days, but previously he spent a week in a less structured program. He was "put down here" under stricter discipline after he got angry and hit someone. The person he got angry with was his mother. The person he hit was his counselor.

Stan lives at home with his mother and two younger brothers. Two older sisters have already left the home, and an older brother is about to move out. Stan's father, whom Stan describes as "one hundred percent Italian and Irish," is in prison, and Stan hasn't seen him since he was six years old. Stan says that his father "drinks a lot and does cocaine. And he's violent."

Stan's mother is part native American, part black. She used to smoke marijuana, drink alcohol and do speed with his father, but now she is sober and has a regular job.

Stan describes himself as chemically dependent. Smoking crack gave him a numb feeling. He wanted more the next day. "I liked the feeling," he says. "I was high and unstoppable." Stan also drank alcohol. He preferred beer to hard liquor. Beer was easier to get.

"I went to high school and got involved with the wrong people," he says. "We were smoking and drinking beer every day. My girlfriend smoked dope. Her friends did, too—only more."

Stan figures to be in treatment another thirty days or

so and then to return to his mother and to his sober friends—"hopefully," he adds. "It's good for me to be here. I finally started talking—opening up." For Stan, and the many others like him, life has become a slippery, day-to-day proposition.

"A lot of people think I'm smart, but that I don't apply myself," he says. "I get good grades. I'm soft and caring when I want to be. Drugs made me angry. I'm afraid to go back to school. They think I'm a druggie—a violent person—a stupid kid who started fights."

Who's to blame for Stan's drug problem?

"Me," he says, "not my father."

Who's in control of his life?

"Me," he responds quickly and unequivocally. "I feel better about myself. I'm talking."

Stan would like to finish high school, go to college and then become a cop, but he's afraid that his past has labeled him. His police record, for example. Once he was arrested for burglary and spent two days in a juvenile detention center.

Stan's past "attitude" and drug problems are intimately tied in with his confusion about his racial status. In his looks and speech, Stan reveals traces of both his mother's black and Indian heritages and his father's Italian and Irish heritages. Stan struggles within an ambiguous racial zone to overcome the negative messages that a racist society tries to force on him.

Beverly

Like the other kids in this chapter, Beverly is categorized by care professionals as a "mid-level" case. She is not yet considered a hardcore, incorrigible user, but she is a lot further along than a beginner. She has been in treatment now for ten of the thirty days she has been scheduled for, one of those weeks being the obligatory week of evaluation. She doesn't know at this time if she'll return home or be placed in a foster home when she is released.

Beverly first sampled alcohol at age twelve, egged on by an older boyfriend. She got "buzzed," liked it and continued to drink with him and his adult friends in order to "gain acceptance." She also tried pot for the first time at age twelve, again with older guys.

At age fifteen, Beverly tried acid. "Everybody was doing it," she says. She bought a hit for five dollars. "It was powder in paper that you put in your mouth to suck." The trip made her laugh. It was fun.

The last couple of trips turned bad, however. She took three hits and suddenly felt that she was covered with black bugs that she couldn't shake off.

"I freaked out," she recalls. "I saw flashing colors. There were streaks." Her head ached miserably, she says, adding: "I also pushed my parents around. They called the cops on me. I had a total change of personality. I hated the feeling of being out of control."

Beverly lives in a mobile home with her natural mother and father and a thirteen-year-old sister. But she's spent a lot of time "on the street." Her mother works in a department store, but her father is unemployed. "I can't go with that," she says, and the subject is not brought up again.

Family Week at the treatment center is just ahead. Beverly and her family have already spent several days discussing their problems openly in preparation for the week-long encounter. Beverly is determined to work on the issues that separate her from her family, but it will be tough. Her difficulty in confronting her father bodes ill for the success of a treatment that hinges on naming and facing all problems squarely.

Beverly has not formally dropped out of school. In fact, she was an "average kid," she says, making B's and C's, until her use of drugs drove her grades down to D's and F's. The drugs gave her a bad attitude. When challenged, Beverly would simply give up on herself, telling the people around her to "bug off"—or worse.

"I didn't think I was worth anything," she says. "I felt I didn't deserve a better life. I was cut down at home and in school. My parents put me down."

Being overweight hasn't helped matters, but, with help, Beverly is beginning to feel better about herself. "Now I'm starting to feel that I'm a good person, no matter what other people think. But I need more positives. I shouldn't cut myself down. And I've got to stop enabling people to get away with things. I want friends badly. I'm willing to protect them at all costs. I didn't have friends until I started using, but those friends used me. I used them. All of us were self-centered. We wanted it, and we wanted it now."

Beverly wants to finish high school and become a legal secretary. "I never had rich stuff like other kids. I was a nerd-type person because of my clothes."

She says that she knows she is chemically dependent.

"I used to blame my dad," she says. "Now I blame myself. I made the choice. It feels good to have a chance to stay sober."

Beverly wants very much to move out of her home, but whatever happens, she'll endure it. She's thinking hard about Family Week. "Nothing's gonna get resolved if we don't talk about it," she says, but she's not sure she can deal with her father. "And Mom," she says mistily, "just goes along with my father."

Rae

Rae will be eighteen on her next birthday, which is old in the world of teenage addicts. A lot has happened to Rae in her short lifetime, and she has a tough, harshly realistic outlook to prove it.

Rae has been in treatment for five weeks now and is due to be released in two more weeks. She transferred into the program from a juvenile detention center. It wasn't until she entered treatment that she found out it wasn't normal to use drugs.

"Everybody in my life uses," she says. "Nobody ever told us drugs were bad."

Rae feels strongly that parents must set a good example for their kids. She comes from a family in which drugs are treated as a matter of fact. Her mother and father both use—cocaine, weed, pills and crack. Her dad does heroin, too. Her brother is in prison for using and dealing drugs. "I never saw a life outside of using," she says.

Was she addicted to crack?

"I still am," she answers.

Rae has a three-year-old boy who is still being cared for by Rae's mother. "He's a little slow because I was using weed when he was born," she says. Another pregnancy ended in miscarriage. The baby's father left when Rae was three months pregnant, but that didn't bother Rae. The young man had been only a casual encounter.

"I'll be chemically dependent for the rest of my life," she says. "I'm just not using right now."

Rae started using drugs because, as she puts it, "it was the thing to do." Everybody she knew used. "I didn't want to be an outcast," she says. A cousin cajoled her into trying drugs the first time, but it really didn't matter who or where or when or how, because drugs were everywhere in her life.

Rae thinks there is hope for her, that she doesn't have to use, that she can stop. She knows what it takes to stay sober. For one thing—perhaps the most important thing—she has to stay away from other people who use drugs, including her own family. For another thing, she has to stay totally clean. "I can't con myself about one use," she admits.

Rae has put herself in the hands of a higher power: Allah. She blames herself for her drug use. "I thought I could stop anytime," she says, "but it didn't matter anyhow. Everybody was addicted. I still want to get high. I feel closer to Mom when we're both high. We're all happy when we're high."

Rae takes a dim view of cops. She describes with anger how cops ripped off her drugs and her brother's guns. She recalls other acts of brutality and racism—cops pushing people around, calling them "niggers" and "welfare junkies" and stealing their property.

Rae's impending release represents a crossroads in her life. If she returns to Mom and Dad, she almost certainly will lapse back into drug use. "I gotta get my own place," she says. Her plan is to go on welfare, get her G.E.D. and then get a job. But the ties that bind her to her past will not loosen easily. Who will care for her baby? How can she hope to avoid her family and using friends entirely? What support groups and services are available to her? What are her chances of changing if the racist society she lives in does not change?

George

"He shouldn't have had me if he didn't love me."

This is how George speaks of a father whose name he doesn't even know.

George entered the treatment program forty days ago. Now he thinks only of going home. Home, for George, is a mother, a stepfather, a stepsister and two stepbrothers.

Prior to entering the program, George had tried to straighten himself out, taking a six-day-a-week job at an amusement park. But he lost the job, and his freedom, when he elected to take a joy ride in a stolen car—his second arrest for auto theft.

At first, George didn't want to quit using drugs. He liked getting high, and he liked doing what he wanted to do—despite the consequences. George was kicked out of school for using marijuana and for skipping classes. He was kicked out of one treatment program for lack of cooperation and out of another for failing to make adequate progress. His attitude was to "blow by, go with the program, get high." He fully expected his drug use to kill him, and yet he didn't care.

Now, he says, he's changed.

George attributes his transformation to his finally being able to admit he has a problem—a problem that he is powerless to combat alone.

"People say I'm mean," he notes defensively. George has been involved in more than one fight over the

114

circumstances of his birth. He knows how to defend himself and survive on the mean streets. Unfortunately, he keeps returning to those streets and to his old friends, all of whom use drugs.

George is a big, sweet, affable sixteen-year-old. Intelligent, adaptable and attentive, he has a promising future ahead of him—if he can beat his drug problem. He admits that he is "in a power struggle" with himself. He says that he wants to return to "a regular school and get a diploma and a job," but he also says he wants to be a professional basketball player. George is a curious mixture of realist and dreamer.

When asked who is to blame for his troubles, George replies: "Myself."

Paul

Paul's bright and easy charm conceals the darker aspects of his personality. Having been sexually abused by a friend's uncle, Paul blithely admits to having abused others. He also admits to occasional acts of violence—for example, shooting out a window in the home of a man who accused him of stealing his son's bicycle.

Thirteen-year-old Paul boasts an I.Q. of 136, but his intelligence was no defense against an alcoholic father who beat Paul and his siblings and who raped his mother twice. Paul's sister, too, was sexually assaulted. It was not easy for Paul's cowed and compliant mother to leave her husband, but she finally found the strength to take her children and flee. By that time, however, Paul had already escaped in his own way, through the use of marijuana and other drugs.

Paul describes his mother as outgoing. Her new

husband is "a nice guy." The description of his stepfather is not as innocuous as it sounds, considering the terror Paul experienced at the hands of his biological father.

Not long after the divorce, Paul's father suffered such severe brain damage in a beating that he cannot ever drink alcohol again without seriously endangering his life. The incident has brought a kind of peace, if only a sullen one, to the troubled family. Paul sees his father as a selfish and sybaritic man, but as is often the case with such kids, he can't wholly separate himself from his abusive parent.

Paul has been in treatment for eighty-nine days. He was put into the program after being arrested for car theft. Paul looks forward to getting out in three weeks, although he doesn't have a very clear notion of what he is going to do then. He credits the program with helping him to confront himself and the things in his life that made him feel shameful, but he's not sure that he can remain sober indefinitely. The drugs made him feel good. He knows now that he can't depend on his intelligence alone to protect him. He must avoid his druggie friends. Return to school. Take things one day at a time. It is the often heard litany of the recovering teenage addict.

At least for Paul, there is the promising stability of his mother's new home.

Tara

Tara and her family have been drowning for years in that most destructive of drugs: alcohol. Her father succumbed to it in 1989, dying from what the doctors said was a heart attack. But Tara knows better. Her mother, two sisters and brother are alcoholics, says Tara matter-of-factly. Tara herself started drinking beer and whiskey at age ten. It helped her to endure the general state of turmoil and instability in her home.

Tara fought often with her family. She physically bullied her mother, finally becoming so belligerent that she had to be taken out the house and placed in a foster home.

Tara would get drunk, offer herself sexually, "do anything" to win the favorable attention of her drinking buddies. Too often afterwards, though, she would come to in the early morning hours of the next day to find herself alone on the streets of the small town where she lived.

"Doing anything" for her "friends" included driving drunk, for which Tara ended up being charged with driving under the influence and driving without a license. Tara knows well the horrors of the drunk tank at the detoxification center even though she only turned fifteen a few months ago.

When asked whom she blames for her problems, Tara names herself without hesitation, and yet she is troubled and confused by many strong, unresolved feelings. Her father's recent death has left her feeling vaguely guilty and disoriented. Toward the mother who abandoned her, she feels resentment. Toward herself, she feels feels shame for her past misbehaviors, anger for her past self-destructiveness, and fear that she may yet return to her old ways.

The seven weeks of treatment have seemed like an eternity for Tara. But now, with her release just four days away, Tara is frightened and unsure. "I don't know if I'll go home. But I just hate the thought of a foster home."

Alcohol still exerts a profound attraction for her. The question for Tara is whether or not the negative consequences of alcohol use will outweigh the pleasure it gives her. "I don't want any more blackouts," she says. Nor does she want to be locked up ever again, no matter how beneficial it may be for her. And she doesn't ever want to find herself wandering the streets alone at night again. "It makes me shake to remember it," she says.

Evelyn

Seventeen-year-old Evelyn is a contemporary example of what used to be called an "incorrigible" case by juvenile authorities. Committing crimes, running away, experimenting with drugs, she has been, for most of her life, at war with the world.

Evelyn has been in treatment for over six weeks. She's not sure what will happen to her when she gets out. She was sentenced to treatment after being convicted of burglary. When the sentence ends, she will be sent to a halfway house and then either to a group home or to her own home. No one is anxious to return her to the dangerous home environment from which she came, but that is where she wants to be.

In Evelyn's family, "everybody drank." Her grandmother died from drink in 1989. Her father is an alcoholic who is "irresponsible and can't hold jobs." Her parents separated when Evelyn was seven years old, and divorced when she was eleven.

An only child, Evelyn calls her father occasionally, but he is unreceptive, even cruel. He tells her that she is "fat, stupid, and a loser" and is "going to jail"—and that's when he's being relatively pleasant. "I always know when he's drinking because then he doesn't want to talk to me at all," Evelyn says. She's not sure whether to cry or to strike back when he abuses her.

Evelyn's mother has also tended to be very critical of her. The lack of positive support at home has exacerbated Evelyn's problems. Lately, her mother has been visiting her in treatment. She appears, finally, to have accepted Evelyn's need for treatment and is attempting to cope with the humiliation she feels for having a child who has been forced into drug rehabilitation.

Evelyn feels good about being sober. She sees the need for finishing school and finding a decent job. She seems determined to succeed. Evelyn blames her father for instigating her drug problems but acknowledges that only she can keep herself sober. "I know I've got to admit my addiction in order to fight it, but I have a hard time with it." She's banking on her mother's developing understanding to help her deal with the daily temptation of returning to drugs.

Joseph

Eighteen-year-old Joseph is a veteran of the juvenile detention and drug treatment systems. After escaping from a Montana treatment center and stealing a car, he was caught and sentenced to the secure lockup of his current treatment program. His problems have blown him like a human tumbleweed across the continent, from the east coast where he grew up to the west to the midwest.

Joseph is an enigma. Mature-looking and athletic, he exudes confidence and gregariousness. He seems a good bet to be popular with his peers. According to

Joseph, both of his parents are "straight and together." His father is employed by a utility company, and his mother teaches. The family lives in a comfortable suburban home.

And yet Joseph is a high school dropout addicted to drugs. And his fifteen-year-old sister is also in treatment for chemical dependency and has attempted suicide.

What was it, then, that led Joseph to use, to become addicted to alcohol, cocaine, pot and acid?

Joseph started using drugs at age eleven. He was curious about alcohol, liked the feeling it gave him. He gravitated toward older friends with whom he could drink and do drugs. It was "a lot of fun getting buzzed," he says, but it "got out of hand." Joseph felt that he needed drugs to get through the day, but when he was high it was "hard to get along with people." He got into many fights.

Joseph is angry at his father for demanding so much from him and for being so inflexible. Joseph has never been able to satisfy his father. In school, C's were unacceptable, and even B's weren't good enough. Whatever Joseph did met with disapproval. His father has yet to visit him in treatment. He's disgusted with his son for messing up. Joseph says that his father is "hard to bullshit."

Joseph doesn't want to go back to using again, but like most of these kids he's not sure if he can stay clean. His two weeks of sobriety in the program have helped him to feel better about himself, but there is always that gnawing doubt and fear.

Whom does Joseph blame for his predicament?

He blames himself first, but he has plenty of blame to pass around: friends, parents, even an overindulgent grandmother who habitually made excuses for behaviors that Joseph now sees were inexcusable.

Joseph is honest and direct. He knows he has messed up, and he is willing to face the consequences of his past actions, but he senses that the time and opportunity to change his life are quickly passing him by.

Harriet

"I've tried everything. Drugs make me happy. This is my third time in treatment. I've been sober four weeks. A guy physically abused me."

Harriet's shattered life is tellingly reflected in these random fragments.

"Mom and Dad drank in front of me a lot," she says. "I stole my first beer at age ten and got sick and puked. My parents were always at the bar."

Harriet feels bad that she got her younger brother drunk when he was seven. He choked on the beer and got scared. She also feels bad that she later enticed him into smoking pot.

Harriet is scheduled to leave treatment two weeks before her sixteenth birthday. She speaks of "having a good life," of staying sober and going to school." "I don't like school, but I want to graduate," she says. She doesn't like school because she doesn't like "getting up in the morning" or "being told what to do." She'd like to get a driver's license and a job and "go on trips with the family." They've promised to take her on a trip to Jamaica if she finishes treatment.

Who controls her life?

"My family."

Who is responsible for her drug use?

"Myself," she replies. "And my family. They were never there for me. I had to take care of my brother."

Harriet has been in treatment just over a month, but she's an old hand, having "run away, done drugs and gotten into trouble with the law."

"I shot up twice with heroin. I was breaking into liquor stores, stealing cars. I joined a satanic cult, stabbed a chick and beat up on my brother and my mom. I was running away all the time. My boyfriend was always hitting me. I was raped by a friend at a party. Eight of my friends died—suicides, car accidents, overdoses. I blacked out a lot. I got angry over nothing." She pauses. "I wish I hadn't done it," she adds.

There have been many consequences from her drug abuse, not the least of which, for her, is forced confinement. "It scares me to be locked up," she says. "I get the feeling I'm going to be locked up forever." She has hurt her family, and more significantly, she has hurt herself. Once she even attempted to kill herself by overdosing on drugs. She knows that she has to think seriously about staying sober. "I have to start liking myself," she says.

Harriet's father is leaving on a trip soon to Las Vegas—to have a "good time." Harriet professes not to be worried about it because he's sober now, but she's not terribly convincing. She's not very convincing about her own sobriety, either. At this point in time, she has no clear vision of the future beyond a driver's license and a trip to Jamaica.

Many factors have combined to shape the negative behaviors of these young addicts: dysfunctional family relationships, peer pressure, inadequate educational, health and welfare programs, harmful and contradictory cultural messages, and countless other environmental (and perhaps biological) determinants. In some cases, the causes and effects of drug addiction seem obvious. In others, they seem extremely subtle or obscure. There's really no reason to expect easy answers given the complexity, range and general unpredictability of human behavior. But that does not mean we can afford to give up on our search for solutions. We have the responsibility as individuals, as family members, as friends and as citizens to understand these factors and to apply remedies as best we can. The future of the nation depends on it.

7

Winning the War on the Home Front

We may be tempted to read the sad stories of the struggling kids in the previous chapter simply as examples of personal failure, failure of individual will. But the stories represent much more than that. They represent the failure of many American institutions—familial, social, cultural and political. In the final chapter of this book, I will offer the outlines of a grand strategy for winning the war on drugs that addresses these failures on a national level. But first I want to take a look at what can be done for our kids on the home front, and I want to start out by focusing on four key areas: family, friends, school and television.

Family

In previous chapters, I talked about the crisis of the American family and the link between that crisis and the drug crisis. The facts are indisputable. The annual number of divorces in the U.S. skyrocketed between 1960 and 1990, rising from 400,000 to 1,200,000. Half of all marriages end in divorce, and studies show that fully one half of all children of divorce suffer long-term trauma, including anxiety and depression. This trauma translates into negative behaviors of all sorts, including drug abuse and addiction.

However adults may justify divorce, children are apt to perceive it as a form of abandonment. Parents need to look at themselves and at their spousal and familial relationships very closely. They especially need to consider the ramifications of divorce in relation to their children's mental and physical well being. Divorce can cure an intolerable situation (alcoholism, drug addiction, physical abuse, compulsive gambling, or similar destructive factors), but it can also cause or exacerbate such problems. Too many divorces in America today occur irresponsibly, for reasons of convenience, and with little concern for the devastating effect such a separation may have on the children involved.

On the other hand, families that stay together don't necessarily stay drug-free together. As I've said before, parents must first look to their own behaviors before they can begin to understand or guide their children's behaviors. Merciless introspection must be the rule, not the exception. Too many parents deny the truth—the truth about themselves and the truth about their children.

Parents must be willing to identify and acknowledge incipient problems and to face them directly. This means treating drug and other addictions as they would a physical malady—by seeking professional help and experienced counseling.

Maybe the best thing that parents can do for their children is simply to listen to them. Nothing is more important, or more problematic, in the parent/child relationship than communication. What parents often forget is that communication is a two-way street. Parents are much better at lecturing their children than they are at listening to them. "I told him a thousand times...I warned her repeatedly about it," parents protest in frustration, and yet the lament of nearly every young addict is: "I could never talk to my parents about my problems." In order for real communication to take place, parents must listen to their children and they must listen to them non-judgmentally and without preconceptions. And, of course, parents must practice what they preach. Their actions must be consistent with and reinforce their words.

Parents also need to provide discipline, accountability and structure in the home by setting reasonable limits and enforcing rules consistently. Overindulgence does spoil. Life visits harsh consequences on all of us, and the best place to learn the hard lessons of life is in a stable, loving, caring home environment. What I'm talking about is similar to what is known in today's jargon as "tough love"—a home where affection is freely given, but where issues of personal responsibility are central and fair rules are strictly enforced.

There are limits to tough love, however, no matter how sincere the motives.

In the summer of 1991, New Yorkers were horrified by the story of a fifteen-year-old Puerto Rican girl named Linda Marrero who had been discovered chained to a radiator in her parents' Bronx apartment. Linda had a long history of drug abuse and addiction. After dropping out of school, she had run away from home repeatedly only to return each time, emaciated and battered, seeking protection from the mean life of the New York City streets. That she continued to survive these escapades seemed miraculous. Meanwhile, her parents had run the bureaucratic gauntlet in search of supervision, counseling, drug treatment, and other types of social services, but had found no help. Finally, in desperation, they chained their daughter to a radiator within reach of a bed, bathroom, television, and stereo.

Two months later the daughter was discovered, and the parents were arrested for unlawful imprisonment—a felony. But as the facts emerged (and Linda herself attested to the love and devotion of her parents), the charges were reduced to a misdemeanor.

This was tough love taken to its dysfunctional extreme, although not so much because the family failed but because the system failed. At the very least, the parents should have been given the opportunity to protect their daughter by putting her into a medical lock-up facility. Stories like this one suggest the limits of what families can do when it comes to protecting themselves against drugs and addiction.

Friends

Young addicts frequently report feelings of inadequacy and low self-esteem. They tend to be loners searching pathetically for companionship and acceptance, and too often they hook up with kids for whom drugs and "friendship" are synonymous. Doing drugs then becomes a vehicle for social acceptance. Exploitation follows and becomes the price for continued "friendship."

Lost in common despair, this club of losers turns inward and nurtures itself on pot, acid, crack, heroin, cocaine, PCP, alcohol, glue and other inhalants, or whatever else comes to hand. The peer pressures are terrific, and the need for acceptance is overwhelming. As the examples in the previous chapter illustrate, these pressures are extremely difficult to overcome.

Over and over again, kids in treatment express their fears and doubts about returning to their old neighborhoods and to their old drug using friends. What hope can they have considering that this is the same enviroment that sparked their addiction and these are the same pressures that they found so irresistible in the past? Clearly, these kids need alternatives—at the very least, a plan that supports their reentry into society by taking such questions seriously into account. We cannot simply throw these children back into dysfunctional relationships and expect them to stay drug-free. Attending a school in a different area, moving to stay with relatives or foster parents, taking a job in a different neighborhood, even joining the armed forces—these may seem like extreme measures, but considering the risks, they may represent less painful alternatives in the long run.

School

A child's world is a series of expanding concentric circles, radiating outward from family to friends to school. Each plays a critical role in the development of the child, and each is a vital point of intervention if we want to prevent children from becoming addicted to drugs.

Many schools are already actively involved in programs of drug prevention and education. National programs like D.A.R.E. (Drug Abuse Resistance Education), a seventeen-week program for fifth and sixth graders taught by specially trained law enforcement officers, and The Partnership for a Drug Free America, which recently announced a $500 million program that included a plan to use fairy tales to convey anti-drug messages to elementary school students, are operating in many districts. Some schools have developed their own programs. In one case, twenty-one fifth graders at a school in Long Branch, New Jersey, produced an anti-drug opera called "What Are We Going to Do?" that dealt directly and honestly with many tough issues in their lives. There are many other similar examples, too numerous to list.

That recent polls indicate a decline in the popularity of hard drugs, at least among some populations, suggests that school programs such as these can and do work. That the same polls reveal an increase in the popularity of legal drugs suggests these programs need to be refined and expanded. Where a prohibitory stance that advocates total abstinence might work for narcotics, it may be relatively ineffective for alcohol. In order to be successful, drug education has to be tailored to the circumstances of use, to the types of drugs used, and to the needs and values of the users and potential users.

The interrelationships between a plethora of social conditions and drug use suggest the need for a more holistic approach to drugs in the schools. Addiction cannot be addressed in isolation from the social factors with which it is linked. Schools need to face issues like teenage pregnancy and high dropout rates squarely by providing sex education, school-based clinics and social welfare support systems for students. Many schools are already doing these things. For example, elementary and middle schools in Beaver County, Pennsylvania have developed an Absentee Prevention Program that tracks student attendance records, identifies those students who are chronically absent from class, analyzes the causes of this absenteeism (lack of academic or social success, anxiety or antagonism toward school, marked behavioral or physiological changes, frequent illness, significant or traumatic event, or negative parental attitudes toward school), and determines an appropriate course of action for correcting the problem. A Madison, Wisconsin program called "Families in Schools Together," reaches out to families with alchohol and drug problems with an eight-week program of weekly multi-family meetings followed by two years of monthly meetings. The program reinforces the child's right to live an alcohol and drug-free life by building communication between parent and child, teaching parenting skills, and providing parents with the assistance and the resources they need to deal with their problems.

All these programs recognize the crucial importance of collaboration and communication between home and school. (Once again we return to the primacy of the family.) For any school-based drug education program to be successful, it is absolutely essential that parents become actively involved in their children's school lives. Even resource-poor school districts can promote such involvement by facilitating parent/teacher associations, open houses, conferences, and other activities that promote frequent and regular communication between home and school.

Television

Television may well be a child's most constant and familiar companion. And yet watching TV, even in a roomful of people, is, paradoxically, a lonely experience because it so absorbs and isolates the viewer. Indeed, television is a very demanding companion, and for that reason—among many others—it is possibly the single most powerful cultural force shaping the values and opinions of children in America today.

What sort of influence does television have on children? In 1981, a number of witnesses before the House Subcommittee on Telecommunications testified to the deep and pervasive influence of television viewing on rising levels of criminality and violence. A 1982 National Institute of Mental Health report concluded that "violence on television does lead to aggressive behavior by children and teenagers." *The New York Times* reported in April 1983 that "there can no longer be any doubt that heavy exposure to televised violence is one of the causes of aggressive behavior, crime and violence in society."

Children imitate what they see on television, and that

includes drug and alcohol use as well as violence and aggression. I've already suggested that television advertising encourages a druggie culture by selling us on the notion that drugs and potions can solve all our problems. The impact of the medium on drug use has been tacitly acknowledged by the passing of laws that forbid the advertising of cigarettes or the drinking of alcoholic beverages on air and by the production and airing of public service campaigns against drugs by the national advertising industry. But we've done very little to control the depiction of drug use, especially licit drugs, in regular programming. What should be done about the depiction of violence and drug use on television? In a democracy like ours that values individual freedoms, censorship is an obnoxious alternative. On the other hand, no right is absolute. We don't, for instance, allow pornography on television. If television programmers cannot practice self-restraint, perhaps they should be restrained by federal laws. The airwaves, after all, are a public resource, regulated in the public interest by the Federal Communications Commission. Surely the American people have the right to demand some balance—some evidence of regard for the influence of program content on impressionable young minds.

What is needed, then, is a coherent and effective policy that governs the depiction of drug use and violence throughout the medium, not only in advertising but in regular programming as well. But until such a policy becomes reality, the burden falls on the home. It's up to parents to exercise guidance and control over their children's viewing habits. Television must be seen as merely a guest in the home, welcome only as long as it behaves properly and doesn't take time away from more

133

useful and valuable activities.

Ideally, it is a stable home that provides the structure that a child needs to stay drug-free. Ideally, concerned parents are the primary agents for ensuring that friends, school and television are positive influences in a child's life. But of course the reality is very often something else: a home that is unstructured or unstable, and parents who are unwilling or unable to influence their children positively. When families fail, it is up to the community at large to step in, whether to support and rebuild the family unit or to provide safe and nurturing alternatives for the children of such families.

Local government, for example, has many more roles to play in this arena than simply the funding and administering of the local school system. As I've pointed out before, government officials need to recognize the differences between short-term palliatives and long-term solutions to major social problems like drug abuse. A community that relies on its criminal justice system as its sole instrument of social policy is not going to solve very many problems in the long run. In fact, it is only going to make those problems worse. If authorities really want to address their local drug and alcohol problems, they're going to have to recognize the importance of providing recreational facilities, treatment centers, training and employment opportunities, and a wide array of other social services for their citizens, especially their younger citizens.

A good example of what I mean is Detroit's Families First, a program that assigns case workers to help families do such things as find housing, learn parenting skills, secure counseling, and get jobs. Another is a new program in Little Rock, Arkansas that will provide free drug and alcohol treatment for any of the city's 26,000 public school students who might need it. Ten local psychiatric hospitals and counseling centers have agreed to charge the school district for the treatment at reduced rates, and a coalition of city officials and community leaders have volunteered to do the fundraising for the project. One final example is the Cafe, a center for teens in Greenwich, Connecticut that holds dances and other drug-free activities for young people under the age of twenty-one. The Cafe stresses an anti-drug philosophy based on personal responsibility and commitment. Although sponsored by the Christ Episcopal Church of Greenwich, it is just the sort of program that local governments should be getting involved in.

Generally, local governments need to treat problems early, upstream, before they become more difficult and costly problems downstream. Specifically, they cannot content themselves with hiring more cops and making more arrests while ignoring less politically appealing but ultimately more effective long-term approaches to the drug problem. There is, of course, an important place for local law enforcement in the war on drugs, but rather than concentrating exclusively on low-level street busts, local law enforcement agencies need to go after the higher-ups in the drug trade the way the Minneapolis Police Department did in the Casey Ramirez case—in coordination with other local and national law enforcement organizations.

Sometimes in the war against drugs there are no clear-cut guidelines for local governments to follow. Such is the case with the issue of intravenous drug use and the government-sanctioned distribution of clean needles. Drug addicts who inject their drugs often share needles, and contaminated needles are a prime culprit in the transmission of the AIDS virus. A Yale University study undertaken in the early 1990s found that government distribution of sterile needles to addicts reduced the spread of AIDS markedly. On the other hand, it can be argued that distributing needles to addicts encourages illicit drug use. At least that's what the city of New York claimed when it scrapped its needle distribution program in 1990. Against the evil of addiction, however, must be balanced what many see as the greater threat of AIDS. The city of New Haven, Connecticut chose to protect against the latter and was able to reduce the incidence of infection in intravenous drug users sharply by distributing free hypodermics. This issue illustrates once again the extreme complexity of the drug problem. It may well be that those politicians who please the masses least—who advocate the least popular policies—are the politicians serving their constituencies best.

Whether individually or collectively, all able members of the community should feel obligated to pitch in and do what they can in the war on drugs. Local businesses, for example, can and should lend their support to initiatives that contribute to the health and welfare of the community at large. Businesses can develop programs to hire and train young people, particularly underprivileged young people. They can grant parental leave to their employees and provide them with daycare facilities. They can sponsor in-house prevention and treatment programs. Many businesses have found that investing in their employees' wellness not only results in a stronger and healthier community, but also improves their bottom line by boosting production and reducing absenteeism.

Many communities are blessed with active volunteer groups, nonprofits, charitable institutions and philanthropic foundations that can and do contribute much to local drug education, prevention and treatment efforts. In addition to effective national organizations like Boys Clubs and Girls Clubs, Boy Scouts and Girl Scouts, and the Y.M.C.A. and the Y.W.C.A., these communities have developed their own local initiatives. The Aroostock Mental Health Center Prevention Project in Caribou, Maine, is one such initiative. It provides prevention training and consultation to community resource representatives and parents, healthy lifestyles training for students, and prevention literature for the entire community. In Lincoln, Nebraska, Community Organizing for Prevention trains local leaders to implement prevention programs in the schools. In Middleburg, Vermont, Alternatives for Teens gives teenagers just that: alternatives to drug use and deliquency. The focus is on getting kids involved in structuring their own programs—social events, weekly meetings, athletic activities. The Leadership Project in Westminster, Vermont selects potential leaders from both high and low risk groups and teaches them leadership skills, respect for differences, and drug prevention strategies, so that the other kids in the community can have many strong positive role models to emulate.

These are only a few of the many initiatives being tried around the country. Much has been done, but clearly much more needs to be done. It is said that people in a democracy get the kind of government they deserve. If citizens are apathetic, their government will be apathetic. But if citizens get involved in their communities, if they vote and communicate with their elected officials, if they form liasons with local law enforcement agencies, if they organize their neighborhoods and schools, if they donate their time and money to making their communities better, then the quality of life improves significantly.

Still, there are many aspects to the drug problem that are too large and intractable to be solved entirely at the local level, especially by those communities that are poor and relatively powerless. How to deal with these larger national and international issues is the subject of the final chapter of this book.

8

Towards a New National Strategy

While much can be done at the local and family levels, the drug problem in America is national in scope. The only way to solve this national drug problem is a concerted approach that reflects the conscious thinking of the entire country. Yet such a unified and consistent view of the problem and its possible solutions is altogether lacking. Current policies constitute a latter-day Tower of Babel in which each state and city speak with distinct and separate voices and each pursues a unique strategy.

There exists little coordination of efforts, scant dissemination of information and a laissez faire attitude from Washington that serves to perpetuate the confusion.

America has demonstrated over and over again its ability to attack and conquer recognized problems. Diseases have been eradicated; social problems have been overcome; issues of environmental concern and consumer protection have been addressed. On the other hand, those problems the nation has refused to or neglected to recognize have tended to fester, deepen, and grow out of control. Drugs and crime are issues that have suffered from neglect—particularly, our neglect of their root causes. At best, we have merely attempted to deal with the symptoms of these problems.

As states continue to stuff their prisons with drug addicts and dealers, the crime and violence fueled by narcotics use and the economies of the trade rise to record levels. Political leaders cite crime statistics selectively. The Bureau of Justice, for example, proclaims a decline in crime against those twelve years old and older from 1973 to 1987, while ignoring the rapidly increasing murder rate. The Bush Administration's current drug czar, Bob Martinez, crows about a decline in hard drug use in America, but he does not mention those ghetto users whose lives are being drastically affected by addiction and violence in epidemic proportions.

By almost all statistical measures over the past twenty years, the circumstances of the nation's poor have worsened. The result has been increasingly unsafe cities, over which hang the clouds of possible riots. By failing to recognize the conditions of life that spawn addiction and crime, the American overclass risks the dissolution of its cities.

The changing demographics, which identify a greater

number of children coming into the population at risk, promise more crime, disorder and violence ahead. Alcoholism and illicit drug use fuel the engines of crime and violence.

The domestic body count in our cities would be unacceptable in any foreign war. Nightly scenes of horror on the news—body bags, manacled prisoners, helicopters whirring overhead and ambulance sirens screaming in the distance—brought a national consensus for action when beamed from Southeast Asia. But in the war that rages on our own streets, we have acquiesced to continued violence with a policy of more cops, tougher enforcement, and bigger prisons without ever analyzing the deep and complex forces behind addiction and crime. It is a tragedy that the underlying causes for our domestic war—poverty and racism—are not discussed. The consequence of this lack of resolution can be seen clearly in the paradigm of Detroit.

On July 23, 1967, a riot started by a police raid on a Detroit after-hours club resulted in forty-three dead. Widespread looting and arson followed. The National Guard was summoned to restore order, but the aftereffects of the violence were significant. Just as 15,000 Bronxites once fled Grand Concourse for Co-op City, those Detroiters who were able to relocated virtually overnight to protected suburban enclaves. By 1987, Detroit's population had shrunk dramatically, from the 1.7 million the city had housed in 1960 to barely 1 million. Also in 1987, Detroit experienced 686 murders, or 63 murders per 100,000 people, one of the worst rates in the nation. This exodus of the overclass from urban areas (often called "white flight") exemplifies how failing to recognize the effects of racial exclusion and economic inequity insure tragic consequences.

President Reagan once observed that in America's war on poverty, "poverty won." During his first term of office, while America's overclass continued to flee its cities, President Reagan touted his tax benefits for the wealthy as "the rising tide which floats all boats." Unfortunately, the small craft remaining in the city of Detroit were swamped and sunk.

Actual data on wealth and poverty in the United States during the twenty-year period of the Detroit example reflects a reduction in the numbers of people living in poverty up until 1975, when the trend reverses. Despite publicized waste and inefficiencies in the poverty programs, America's abandoned war on poverty was anything but a total loss. We can only imagine how much better the results could have been with more careful planning, better implementation and continued popular support. Clear implications exist in this data that reductions in the rate of poverty translate into reduced drug use and criminal behaviors which are rooted in drugs.

Popular support for funding programs to eradicate poverty has dwindled. We Americans like to enterain the fiction that ours is a classless, egalitarian society. Certainly it is more equal than most, especially where legal rights are concerned. Americans are offended by such terms as "overclass" and "underclass," as I have discovered virtually every time I have used the terms. We seem more comfortable with words which have a more individual connotation. We can speak easily of a "rich" person or the "wealthy," but we balk at the term "overclass." With great compassion, charities have raised generous donations for the "needy" or the "poor." But try to pass the hat for the "underclass" and see the difference. Nowadays it seems that even terms like "needy" and "poor" need qualification. Our suspicions of the poor are reflected by such vacuous distinctions as "the truly needy."

I can remember being on a call-in radio show discussing the effects of inequitable distribution of wealth on the crime rate. An irate caller said, "Well, then, doesn't everything you've said come down to a simple call for redistributing our incomes?"

To frame my argument in more confortable and familiar terms, I replied: "What do you think think the tax conferees in Congress are discussing as we speak if not how to distribute income through tax policies?"

It hadn't occurred to the listener, as it wouldn't to so many of his fellow citizens, that we already redistribute our wealth. The only point of contention remains in the allocation. For that we elect Congress.

Members of the overclass, registered to vote, file to their polling places and lobby their elected representatives in Washington's corridors of influence. Their voices are heard.

On the local level, every police executive takes notice of the concerns of the overclass. When a Yale senior was murdered by a mugger, the University President announced, "We will take whatever steps are necessary to protect our campus." (*The New York Times*, February 19, 1991) When an investment broker was assualted by inner city kids "wilding" in Central Park, the entire world's attention focused on the event. Whatever touches the overclass gets addressed in a hurry. And what doesn't affect the overclass suffers neglect.

It is not an accident that the underclass must resort

to civil disobedience and mass demonstration to participate in public debate. The underclass is forced to find alternative ways to focus the attention of the overclass on their plight.

In our supposedly egalitarian society, economic disparity is now at its most extreme in postwar history. One fifth of working Americans earn more money than the remaining four fifths put together. Lowering the income tax rates for upper income brackets has enabled the elite to consolidate and extend their economic dominance. Their concentrated wealth has covered their escape to suburban enclaves and robbed urban centers of critical property tax revenues. The wealthy have taken lucrative jobs, fully funded schools and recreational facilities with them. The overclass even hires private guards to police its communities.

Some political leaders have paid dearly for their quixotic efforts to remedy economic imbalances. Governor James Florio of New Jersey attempted to equalize school expenditures between the poorly funded and richly endowed systems through a process of redistribution of tax revenue. The fury loosed on Florio and his political allies far exceeded the normal bounds of political disagreement. He has since found it prudent to trim his sails and tack the prevailing wind. He learned quickly to accommodate the overclass in both his words and actions. Governor Florio's experience is a cautionary tale, spelling out dramatically the pain awaiting those who would champion the interests of the poor.

The most pressing issues for America's underclass are drugs and crime. While the overclass reports a diminution in illegal drug use, the underclass continues to use drugs as an escape from the realities of life. I have tried to make the case in this book that unchanging and harsh reality hardens experimental or occasional drug use to addiction—and to a spiral of violence and despair.

The flight from the cities to the suburbs by the overclass may well afford the wealthy only temporary respite from the problems of drugs and violence in our cities. The fate of the overclass—and our fate as a nation—is tied to the survival of our urban centers.

Three quarters of all crime and violence in the United States is connected to drug and alcohol use. In 1990, America had over 750,000 inmates in prision and over a million behind bars, including the local jails, where the majority of those incarcerated were awaiting trial. We now lead the world—passing South Africa and the Soviet Union—in per capita incarceration rates. Our murder rate is about seven times that of European countries and rising. Our prison population doubled in the last decade, jumping over 54% from 1980 to 1987 alone. This trend of incarceration shows a panicky reaction to drug-related crime and our foolish determination to lock up every junkie. Overwhelmingly, the prison population is made up of those who have committed drug-related crimes. California officials estimate that 85% of the convicts entering their prison system have a substance abuse problem. When America recovers from its drug addiction, we will become a dramatically safer society.

Our recovery will be based on our collective ability to admit we have a problem and to explore the root causes of our addiction. The deep and growing economic chasm between the overclass and the underclass must be bridged. The illiterate must be educated, the jobless put back into the workforce. Health care must be universally and freely available.

For conservatives who insist on accountability, punishment and individual responsibility while decrying the folly of free lunches, chapter six is full of the recovering person's references to the healing importance of "consequences." Illicit drug use, despite what some may claim, is not a victimless crime. When children are abused, neglected and abandoned; when families become splintered and impoverished; when innocent bystanders are assaulted, robbed and murdered, it is absurd to argue that drugs harm only the user and that we should be more tolerant of drug use. For our nation to recover fully from the diseases of drugs and violence, there must be both inducements and sanctions.

Housing, employment, health care and education must be provided for all citizens, and the recipients must both remain responsible for their individual actions and expect penalties for breaches of the standards imposed by the state. Even those Americans who are suspicious of government and dubious of its capacity to play a useful role in our daily lives must understand that the state does have a obligation to dispense resources and to insure the proper and appropriate use of those resources.

America, through its unfair tax and wealth distribution policies, has created the most economically polarized society of any industrialized nation. Overall, we provide our citizens the fewest health, welfare and social services. Economic inequities consign large numbers of citizens to poverty and exclusion from participation in the "American Dream."

Rearranging the tax structure and diverting funds from the defense budget to social programs would benefit the nation in many ways. Not the least of these benefits would be to reengage the overclass—financially and personally—in the solutions to the problems created by drugs, poverty and racism which plague our cities.

We must see that our government is not only better managed but that it is given a stronger role to play in reordering the collection of revenues and the allocation of benefits. Only through accountability can we rebuild our confidence that our resources are well spent and effectively managed.

If poverty and racism are to be attacked successfully, the issues must be debated comprehensively. The absence of debate has resulted in a vacuum that has been filled by speculation and instant cures. Instead of thoughtful discussion from which a national consensus might grow, we harbor vain hopes of skewering our social problems with a single, deft stab. There are no better examples of this lack of informed debate than our "solutions" to the drug problem, including the call for decriminalizing "hard" (mostly felony possession) drugs.

The arguments for making possession and use of crack, cocaine, heroin and marijuana non-crimes are wide-ranging. Many cite the failure of the war on drugs: the supply of illegal drugs remains plentiful and the low prices indicate the ease of traffic in this contraband.

Proponents of decriminalization say that the state would be able to control dosages and monitor addicts to prevent the spread of drugs and the diseases connected to drug use. Drug users would also be free of the economic dilemma of sustaining an expensive habit, since drugs would be available at a much lower cost. And the crimes connected to the drug trade—turf wars and battles for control—would miraculously vanish along with the profits of the criminal element. We weren't able to control alcohol during Prohibition, right? And Prohibition led to the rise of organized crime. Since alcohol and tobacco—our two deadliest drugs—are legal, then why not other drugs?

Then there is the libertarian-style argument that drugs harm only the user; individuals should be free to make the choice. Finally, there are the fiscally prudent arguments that the criminal justice system would be free to deal with more serious crimes, and that drugs could be taxed, with proceeds going to prevention, education, and treatment programs.

It must be said that some very prominent, usually clearheaded thinkers support the above arguments. In fairness, some of the positions are not devoid of reason. But it is significant that the International Association of Chiefs of Police, the largest organization of police executives in the world, has repeatedly condemned legalizing hard drugs. Individual police chiefs from our largest cities have rejected the notion of decriminalization, even as they acknowledge their frustrations and the lack of progress in the war on drugs.

When setting any social policy, we must keep in mind that the state does have a duty to protect its citizens. The Food and Drug Administration carefully tests and evaluates substances intended for our ingestion. It is indisputable that drugs can cause addiction and produce enormous bodily harm. As a pharmacological effect, some drugs also produce erratic behaviors in certain users, leading to criminal acts.

Legalization has been attempted in the past and abandoned as unworkable. Drug use tends to increase when drugs are legalized. Legalization means that the state has declared that drugs are okay. Therefore, decriminalization is not a value-neutral action. Since we as citizens assign the state the function of protecting us from harmful substances, legalization represents a de facto stamp of approval for drug use.

The nations of the world generally agree that hard drugs are harmful, and most have declared them contraband. The United Nations has adopted many reports which acknowledge the evil of hard drugs and call for their elimination. America would stand virtually alone in the international community if it broke ranks on this issue.

Some experts favor simply adopting a moratorium on enforcement rather than changing the laws. There seems to be a measure of hypocrisy in that approach. Our policy should always be to have our laws reflect our societal values and to enforce all laws equally. To do any less would encourage disrespect for the law.

For all the arguments against it, however, decriminalization is an idea worth debating. At the very least we should consider substituting treatment for tougher penalties—in essence, treating drugs more as a public health problem than a criminal justice problem, the way the Netherlands does (and does successfully). Or we might even consider something like the plea bargain approach of the current Columbian government, which I'll explain later; it is certainly analagous to decriminalization. Whatever we may think of the idea, any examination of America's drug problem must include all possibilities, giving each one careful consideration.

Another strategy for winning the drug war put forth by the quick-fixers is the currency strategy, which was described by Donald T. Regan, President Reagan's Treasury Secretary and later his Chief of Staff, in *The New*

York Times on September 18, 1989. Mr. Regan proposed withdrawing all $50 and $100 bills from circulation and replacing them with secretly printed new ones. This would, supposedly, leave the drug lords stuck with piles of worthless notes. How feasible is this strategy?

On January 23, 1991, the Soviet Union ordered the immediate surrender of all 50 and 100 ruble notes (the highest denomimations). The notes were to be exchanged for smaller denominations, up to a limit of 1000 total rubles. The 50 and 100 ruble notes were to be worthless within three days.

This drastic measure on the part of the Soviets was aimed at curbing inflation by reducing the money supply and cutting back the burgeoning black market that had relied on large notes for its transactions. Sadly, the gambit wiped out savings and caused panic, chaos and anger. The currency strategy led to some Russian republics defying Moscow and to the extension of the exchange deadline until February 1, 1991.

Large-scale currency exchanges have been proposed and implemented for different reasons in recent years. In his 1991 book, *Drugs in America*, Vincent Bugliosi suggests the creation of two separate currencies—one for domestic and one for foreign use. The present currency would be legal outside the United States but worthless within the country. Laws would be passed restricting the rights of travelers to exchange U.S. dollars for foreign monies. Banks, being the lynchpins of the laundering operations, would have federal agents in residence to monitor major transactions and question clients with large amounts of cash. This system, with its complications, inconveniences and hardships, seems more likely to paralyze international commerce than to seriously hamper drug dealers who can purchase the highest priced talents to circumvent operations which could hobble the less well-heeled.

The currency strategy does not look at the root causes of drug use and addiction, nor does it even attempt to address the most rudimentary issues of supply and demand. It is hard to believe that any responsible public official would take this course of action any more seriously than Donald Regan's "lightning obsolescence," suggested three years ago.

For some quick-fixers, there is always the military option. The invasion of Panama by United States forces on December 20, 1989 was ostensibly another battle in our war on drugs. The leader of Panama, Manuel Antonio Noriega, was accused of drug trafficking by the United States. He was removed from power and brought to Florida to stand trial. (The widely heralded seizure of drugs at Noriega's residence, however, turned out to be tamale mix.) The invasion was justified to the American people as necessary to combat drug trafficking. Sadly, by August 1991, Panama had made a comeback as a prime transshipment point between growers in the Andes and users in the Bronx. The DEA reported average monthly cocaine seizures by Panamaian officials at 316.9 pounds in 1989; 725.0 pounds in 1990; and 1,892.3 pounds through June of 1991. The drug continues to arrive by plane and boat from Columbia into Panama, where it is then shipped to Mexico and spirited into the United States. Authorities estimate that 70% of the cocaine reaching the United States enters in this fashion.

While the 1989 invasion shows less than perfect results, the fact remains that drugs are an international problem and require international cooperation and response.

In August 1991, the Bush Administration announced that military personnel would be sent to Peru. Acting as advisors to the Peruvians, U.S. personnel would set up two combat batallions, help create a river patrol force, refurbish army helicopters and combat jets, and help reform the Peruvian military justice system. Since the Bush Administration estimates that Peru produces 70% of the world's cocaine, it is hoped that a stronger Peruvian army could protect police units involved in interdiction and eradication operations.

Washington set up similar training programs in Bolivia and Columbia. All of these efforts have been undertaken with the consent of the host governments, but the use of United States military advisors creates a delicate political situation.

In Bugliosi's *Drugs in America*, the author suggests what even what the most jingoistic and gung ho war hawks in Washington would hesitate to offer as a possible strategy: unilateral invasion of cocaine-producing nations to attack drug lords. Making the case that the interdiction and eradication efforts of our Latin American neighbors haven't worked, Bugliosi offers "a very limited search and find mission by that number of military personnel deemed necessary by the Joint Chiefs of Staff to accomplish the job."

In case this euphemistic language obscures his meaning, Bugliosi explains further: "If, for whatever reason, the Colombian government would not authorize our military intervention, then we should intervene without their blessing. There is ample legal and constitutional justification for such an action."

What Bugliosi is suggesting is the creation of a sort

of "Invasion of the Month" program, which would conceivably include the countries of Peru and Bolivia. Once a course of military intervention such as Bugliosi envisions is begun, what would prevent the countries of Mexico, Afghanistan or Thailand from becoming targets for our intervention?

Despite the temptation to use force, and even its occasional efficacy, can anyone take such a proposal seriously?

The war on drugs did become a literal war on the streets of Columbia's cities during the late 1980s. Explosions, assasinations, gun battles and mass murders paralyzed the country. Eleven Supreme Court Justices were murdered on November 6, 1985, over the issue of supporting an extradition treaty that would have resulted in Columbian drug lords being sent to the United States to face charges and possible imprisonment.

Three of Columbia's presidential candidates were assassinated in 1990. Hundreds of cops were killed for the $4,300 bounty offered by drug barons. Journalists were intimidated and newspaper offices blown up. An Avianca airliner, carrying 110 passengers, exploded in flight, killing all aboard.

It was America's insatiable demand for drugs that created the billionaire drug kingpins who financed insurrection against the Columbian government. Political killings in Columbia were estimated at 2,500 in 1989-1990 alone.

Following the failure of the crackdown on drug kingpins by his predecessor, President Virgilio Barco, Columbia's succeeding President, César Gaviria, who ran for office on a strongly anti-drug-cartel platform, promised no extradition for drug dealers who surrendered and pleaded guilty to one crime. The sentences would be light, prison time short. The traffickers were still not satisfied. They wanted amnesty. Eight journalists were kidnapped. Gaviria held firm to his offer, however, and the drug lords relented, agreeing to the provisions set forth in his program. One kingpin who surrendered under this policy served two months and was set free by a judge who later resigned.

Under renewed threat of extradition to the United States, the most violent and widely sought trafficker, Pablo Escobar, surrendered and was flown to a country club-style prison, set up especially for him, in his hometown. Other members of his notorious Medellin Cartel surrendered with him.

Escobar, a multibillionaire, faced ten indictments in the United States for drug trafficking and murder. He was believed to have showered gifts on his hometown—rent-free apartments, food baskets, unemployment and health insurance, and scholarships. The prison in his hometown was built to his specifications. Because of his fear of retaliation from the associates of cops he had murdered, a contract governed who was allowed to enter his prison. The town's mayor visited Escobar on his first night there, and the two watched the news together. Escobar's mother, of course, was given free access. All the efforts of the cartels are geared toward avoiding American justice as Escobar did.

The Columbian government's new surrender/no-extradition policy is not popular among American officials. The Columbian justice system is in disarray, and there is little confidence in its workings. However, American leaders are reluctant to openly criticize any efforts of the Columbians to deal with the crimes and punishments of drug kingpins. It is too early to assess President Gaviria's program, although we do know that in the first nine months of 1991 violence has abated dramatically and cocaine seizures have risen significantly. Also, there is an obvious benefit to having drug kingpins behind bars when they might otherwise be operating freely. President Gaviria's initiative deserves thoughtful evaluation before any definitive conclusion can or should be drawn.

America must turn its critical gaze to our own national strategy. We must determine how to allocate our own human and material resources to attack this nation's seemingly insatiable demand for drugs.

A presidential commission on drug abuse is needed. The Bush Administration has been content up to this point to throw green at the demand for drugs, so that the local governments can throw blue at it. The federal drug budget clearly reflects a preference for spending money on overtime and salaries for more cops to make more arrests. Rather than continuing this one-sided emphasis on law enforcement personnel, the presidential commission I am proposing would be balanced with experts in health and social services, education and related fields, and would be given sufficient time and resources to produce a comprehensive strategic plan. This commission would be charged with looking at the problem of demand for drugs and with seeking changes in how we currently enforce our national and local laws against the supply of illegal drugs.

A new plan for more effective interdiction, suppression and elimination of the supply of illegal drugs would depend on an investigation of the prosecutorial avenues available to the criminal justice system. Enforcement experts should openly discuss the collection of intelligence relating to all aspects of drug trafficking. Even failed investigations produce valuable information. This data must be collected in a central repository for future inquiries.

Enforcement efforts must concentrate on higher-ups. Local jurisdictions need technical training and support in the use of undercover operators, infiltrators, wiretaps, search warrants, and other investigative approaches. The quality of enforcement should be uniformly high throughout the nation. Federal/local partnerships can multiply the current resources of money, equipment and personnel. This joint approach overcomes the geographic limitations that keep most of America's cops within the narrow confines of city boundaries.

The Drug Enforcement Agency is ideally positioned for the important coordinating role necessary for joint operations. Although subjected to a hostile merger with the Federal Bureau of Investigation in the mid-1980s, the DEA has nonetheless been the lead agency in prosecuting the war on drugs. Naturally, the DEA will have to employ the expertise of other departments and agencies—the State Department, for example, to negotiate and initiate diplomatic efforts, and the FBI and local enforcement agencies to address specific enforcement priorities. There is no area of policing where the contrast between pleasing the public and serving them effectively is as clearly etched as in narcotics operations. Priorities must be set and addressed through coordinated efforts.

In the area of education, this commission on drug abuse must sift through the mixed messages the nation receives about drug use and develop a more coherent approach. The message of drug abuse must be broadened beyond the formal, lecture-style format and incorporated into the areas of the culture most likely to reach the young. Commission educators need to evaluate existing programs (D.A.R.E, "Just Say No," various local initiatives, and others) with a critical eye on evidence of each program's effectiveness.

Treatment professionals from the health and social service fields will add their expertise in the fields of addiction and recovery. The treatment area is currently starved for resources. Only a fraction of addicts seeking treatment are able to find it. New York State spent $1.5 billion building prisons in the 1980s, providing only 5,000 beds for inmate drug treatment. As a result, thousands of New York's 55,000 prison inmates must wait months for treatment of their addiction. Providing treatment to prisoners such as these would not only improve the overall conditions within prisons, but also inhibit a return to the lifestyle that produced their criminal behavior in the first place.

Information sharing by treatment centers is necessary, and more researchers need to be drawn into the field to develop and evaluate the wide variety of approaches. The values of resident programs, total abstinence, frequent testing and self-help programs should be considered and compared. As in both drug enforcement and drug education, a what-works-and-what-doesn't standard to treatment of America's drug problem must be applied.

The most effective way to attack addiction is to prevent a kid from experimenting with drugs in the first place, and so the commission on drug abuse I am proposing would be assigned to develop a comprehensive prevention program as one of its first priorities. We already know that in the near future we will be forced to cope with widespread behavioral problems caused by drug addiction. Any prevention strategy would have to include intense educational programs designed for teenagers, especially in the areas pregnancy prevention, prenatal care, and parenting skills. The more evidence that accumulates concerning the problems of babies born to addicted mothers, the clearer the importance of early intervention by health professionals becomes as a drug abuse prevention strategy.

Drug abuse undeniably produces antisocial "monsters," and these monsters must be punished, even as we come to understand the reasons for addictive behaviors. On these pages I have described a disease for which violence is merely a symptom. For some people with this disease there will be no recovery; for others, rehabilitation and reassimilation will occur. But our policy of dealing only with the predators or recidivists has merely resulted in swelling their numbers in our prisons. We have to look at crime from its beginnings.

The abuse of drugs, criminal behavior, teenage pregnancy and increasing violence are interconnected and have roots in the conditions of life forced on the underclass by the overclass.

The government has a role to play to insure the quality of the lives of all its citizens. It has the right to protect its citizens from anything which threatens the country's internal or external peace, but it also has the responsibility to do all it can to eliminate the sources of crime and violence. The government also has the responsibility to redistribute income through taxation and disbursement and to make sure that collective resources are used effectively.

The war on poverty must be refought. Care, love, and attention nourish lives of beauty and productivity. Brutality, scorn, and exclusion starve human life. Our drug problem requires a commitment to change that begins with concern for the needs of the poor, the young, the homeless and the excluded.

Our democracy should reflect the wishes, hopes, ambitions, and values of all the American people. We can no longer afford the attitude so prominent in the last decade: to get rich and have a good time, and let today's poor and tomorrow's children pay the freight. Rather, we must relearn the values of generosity, compassion, and altruism, and reinstill these values in our children. These values must be communicated not only through our homes, schools, and churches, but through the mass media, and by example in the actions of our local and national leaders.

Temple Israel
Minneapolis, Minnesota

IN MEMORY OF
JOSEPH BROUDE
FROM
MILDRED GENDLER

Index

Abortion, and children of addiction, 52-54. *See also* Addiction; Blacks; Children; Poverty
Absenteeism. *See* Schools
Abuse of drugs, root of, 16
Acceptance, need for, 129
Accountability, 127, 146, 147
Acid. *See* LSD
Addiction. *See also* Poverty; Treatment
  babies of, 35, 47-48
  biological connection, 58-61
  consumerism, 66-68
  contributing factors, 59-60, 123, 131
  and crime, 34-35
  cultural factors, 66-69
  cycle of, 35
  and decriminalization, 148-149
  defined, 55-56
  denial of, 64-65
  and divorce, 126
  and education, 69-70, 130-131
  epidemic of, 140
  families and, 47-54
  and police, 35-40
  and pop music, 68-69
  and prisons, 70-73
  role models, 61-63, 67-69
  root of, 145
  signs of, 56
  treatment, 65
  triggers of, 65-70

Twelve Step Programs, 65
Afghanistan, 25, 30
African-American. *See* Black
AIDS, 40, 45, 60, 77, 136
Alcohol, 2, 92, 97, 98, 101, 103, 108, 110, 115, 116, 120
  and children, 3
  and divorce, 126
  as escape, 18
  link to crime, 70-71
  reasons for using, 77 (fig.)
  and television, 133
  use in past year, 82 (fig.)
Alcoholics Anonymous, shortcoming of, 65
Alternatives for Teens, Middleburg (VT), 157
Amanda's story, 98-101
Amphetamines, 75, 82 (fig.), 108
  and crime, 71, 98, 103
Angel dust, 75
  and crime, 71
Aroostock Mental Health Center Prevention Project, Caribou (MA), 137
Assault, 33. *See also* Children; Misogyny; Sexual molestation; Violence

Barbara's story, 105
Barbiturates, 75
Barco, Virgilio, President (Columbia), 153
Bennett, William, 9-11
Beverly's story, 109-112
Blacks, 23. *See also* Color, people of
  alienation, feelings of, 45

161

and crime, 34-35
dealers, 40
distribution, 25-26
and friends, 129
origin, 26, 152
police use of, 37-38
poverty, use in, 41
schools, use in, 42 (fig.)
Color, people of, 17
Columbia, 7, 14, 26, 30, 149, 151-155
Communication, 30-31
in families, 127
Community based prevention programs. *See* Alternatives for Teens; Aroostock Mental Health Center Prevention Project; Business; Children's Defense Fund; Community Organizing for Prevention; D.A.R.E.; Daycare; Detroit Families First; Dysfunctional; Education; "Families in Schools Together"; Family; Leadership Project; Operation Pressure Point; Political; Prevention
Community Organizing for Prevention, Lincoln (NE), 137
Congenital problems from drugs. *See* Children
Connecticut, 22
Consequences. *See* Accountability
Conservative
measures, 10
and Supreme Court decisions, 19
Constitutional rights, 17

Consumerism and substance abuse, 66-68
Contraceptives, 85-86. *See also* Abortion; AIDS; Children
Corporate sector, 13
Crack, 18, 26, 75, 112. *See also* Children; Cocaine
and crime, 34-35
families and, 47-54
friends and, 129
and sexual abuse of children, 48
Crime. *See also* Addiction; Amphetamines; Angel dust; Blacks; Burglary; Cartels; Central Intelligence Agency; Children; Coast Guard; Cocaine; Columbia; Community based programs; Crack; Dealers; Decriminalization; Defense Department; Detroit; Drug Enforcement Agency; Employment; Enforcement; Federal; Federal Bureau of Investigation; Heroin; International Association of Chiefs of Police; Judicial system; Military; Money; Mugging; Murder rate; Music; Netherlands; Noriega; PCP; Police; Poverty; Prison; Racism; Ramirez; Sentencing; Sexual; Strategy; Street; Television; Underclass; Victims; Violence
and drugs, 1, 33, 46, 140-141, 145
organized, 11
Cultural heroes, 4-5. *See also*

Education. *See* D.A.R.E.

Drug Enforcement Agency (DEA), 12, 30, 151, 156

Drugs in America, Vincent Bugliosi, 150, 152.

Dysfunctional. *See also* Alcohol; Addiction; Detroit Families First; "Families in School Together"; Government Assistance; Violence
extreme, 128
families, 122-123

Education. *See also* Intervention points; Prevention; Strategy
and blacks, 43-44
drug, 13-14, 157-158
from drug tax, 148
parenting, 158
prenatal, 158
and recovery, 145
sex, 85-86
strategy, 155-157

Employment opportunities, 134, 135, 145, 146. *See also* Poverty

Enforcement, 13, 15, 17, 26-31. *See also* Bureau of Justice; Central Intelligence Agency; Coast Guard; Constitutional Rights; Dealers; Federal; Intelligence; Judicial system; Military; Money; Plea bargaining; Police; Policy; Prison; Sentencing; Street

Escobar, Pablo, 154

Europe, 23, 25

Evelyn's story, 118-119

"Families in School Together," 131

Family. *See also* Children; Detroit Families First; Dysfunctional; "Families in School Together"
crisis in, 126
focus on, 1
introspection as guide, 126
limits of, 128
structure, 127
support for, 134

Federal. *See also* Government assistance; State Department
Bureau of Investigation (FBI), 12, 156
Center for Disease Control (CDC), 40
Communications Commission, 133
employee assistance program, 13, 19
enforcement, 11, 20-22
money, 11
task force, 11

Fiscal argument, 148

Florio, Governor James (NJ), 144

Food and Drug Administration (FDA), 148

Friends. *See also* Children; Street gangs
alternatives, 129
drugs and, 129

Gamblers Anonymous, shortcoming of, 65

Gangs, *See* Street

Gaviria, César, President (Co-